D0214003

LEFTOVER WOMEN

The resurgence of gender
inequality in China

LETA HONG FINCHER

Zed Books

LONDON

Leftover Women: The Resurgence of Gender Inequality in China was first published in 2014 by Zed Books Ltd.

This edition first published 2016.

Zed Books Ltd, The Foundry, 17 Oval Way, London SE11 5RR, UK.

www.zedbooks.net

Copyright © Leta Hong Fincher 2014

The right of Leta Hong Fincher to be identified as the author of this work has been asserted by her in accordance with the Copyright, Designs and Patents Act, 1988.

Designed and typeset in Bembo Std by seagulls.net
Index by John Barker
Cover design by Steven Marsden

All rights reserved. No part of this publication may be reproduced, stored in a retrieval system or transmitted in any form or by any means, electronic, mechanical, photocopying or otherwise, without the prior permission of Zed Books Ltd.

A catalogue record for this book is available from the British Library.

ISBN 978-1-78360-789-1 pb
ISBN 978-1-78360-790-7 pdf
ISBN 978-1-78360-791-4 epub
ISBN 978-1-78360-792-1 mobi

Printed and bound by CPI Group (UK) Ltd, Croydon, CR0 4YY

MIX
Paper from
responsible sources
FSC® C013604

For Mike, Aidan and Liam

Contents

Introduction

Li Fang* is relieved that she found a husband just in the nick of time. The parents of the university graduate and former human resources manager in Beijing feared that their only daughter was getting old and might never be able to marry. Li worried that she would pass the "best child-bearing age" and might no longer be able to give birth. She is 26.

Just after marrying, Li lost her job because her company did not want her to take two weeks of unpaid leave for a honeymoon. She does not share a bank account with her husband and does not know how much is in his account. Yet Li does not wish to discuss finances with her new husband now that she is unemployed, for fear that the topic would "hurt his feelings." Rather than ask her husband to share more of his spending money with her, she is drawing down her own savings to pay for groceries, transportation and clothing. She also feels she has no claim to ownership of the marital home she shares with her husband because the home is registered in his name alone.

"I do not have the right to expropriate property from someone else's family," says Li. So marriage does not provide Li with any

---

*In order to ensure the anonymity of interviewees, most names in the book are pseudonyms, and in some cases minor details of an interviewee's profession have been altered. All translations are my own.

shared ownership of assets, property or income, even though she lost her job precisely because she got married: why, then, does Li consider herself lucky? Well, she avoided the fate of her good friend, an executive at a multinational company who earns a top salary, but is still single at 31 years old and therefore branded a "leftover" woman.

"Several men have pursued her, but she's not willing to marry them because her standards are too high. If she carries on like this, she will never find a husband," says Li.

Something is wrong with this picture.

In China, the derogatory term "leftover" woman or *shengnü* (剩女) is widely used to describe an urban, professional female in her late twenties or older who is still single. Many urban Chinese women, like Li, express anxiety about becoming a "leftover" woman if they are not married by their late twenties. And many marry quickly – often within several months of meeting a man – specifically to avoid being designated "leftover." The intense pressure to marry comes from parents, relatives, friends and colleagues. But this pressure is magnified multiple times by the Chinese state media and government-sponsored matchmaking events.

Even the state feminist agency, the All-China Women's Federation, has perpetuated the "leftover" women term. China's ruling Communist Party established the Women's Federation to "protect women's rights and interests." The emancipation of women was a key goal of both the Communist Revolution, which culminated in the founding of the People's Republic of China in 1949, and, decades before that, of the Republican Revolution, which toppled the country's last dynasty, the Qing (1644–1911). Yet the Women's Federation today has taken a leading role in the campaign to pressure urban, educated women in their mid- to late twenties to stop being so ambitious and get married.

In 2007, the Women's Federation defined the term "leftover" women as single women older than 27, according to the state-run Xinhua News Agency, the official mouthpiece of China's Communist Party. That same year, China's Ministry of Education added the term to its official lexicon. Since then, the Chinese state media have aggressively promoted the term through articles, surveys, cartoons and editorials stigmatizing educated women who are still single, often referring to a "crisis" in growing numbers of educated women who "cannot find a husband."

Typical headlines run by Xinhua News scream like sensational tabloids: "Overcoming the Big Four Emotional Blocks – Leftover Women Can Break out of Being Single"; "Eight Simple Moves to Escape the Leftover Women Trap," and the column "Do Leftover Women Really Deserve Our Sympathy?", which was posted on the Women's Federation website in March 2011, just after International Women's Day:

> Pretty girls don't need a lot of education to marry into a rich and powerful family, but girls with an average or ugly appearance will find it difficult. These kinds of girls hope to further their education in order to increase their competitiveness. The tragedy is, they don't realize that as women age, they are worth less and less, so by the time they get their M.A. or Ph.D., they are already old, like yellowed pearls.

This brazenly insulting statement may have come from the Chinese state media, but its message of gender discrimination is all too familiar for many women in other parts of the world who encounter some of the same obstacles facing Chinese women.

This book argues that the state-sponsored media campaign about "leftover" women is part of a broad resurgence of gender inequality in post-socialist China, particularly over the past decade and a half of market reforms. I focus on urban, educated, emerging middle-class women in China. Yet I have received messages through my Twitter account from women in countries such as India, Pakistan, Russia, Turkey, Singapore, Nigeria, Kenya and the Philippines telling me that they, too, face intense pressure to marry and stigma if they remain single. Women in highly industrialized countries such as the United States and Great Britain share some of the same problems of gender inequality in wealth now experienced by women in modern China. I hope that this book will speak to readers everywhere.

In China, the world's most populous country, gender-discriminatory norms are exacerbated by a one-party state intent on social engineering, with a massive propaganda apparatus that maintains a tight grip on information and whose goals increasingly go against those of women.

The Chinese word *"sheng"* (剩) refers mainly to leftover or spoiled food, which must be discarded. When used in relation to women, the term adds to the emotional resonance of China's mass media campaign. The irony of this campaign to denigrate single women is that China's one-child policy, preference for sons, and widespread abortion of female fetuses have caused a surplus of *men* due to the severe sex-ratio imbalance, which the State Council calls "a threat to social stability." The official Communist Party newspaper, the *People's Daily*, writes that millions of men unable to find wives are more likely to take part in "rioting, stealing and gang fighting." China's National Bureau of Statistics data at the time of writing show that there about 20 million more men under 30 than women under 30.

Some economists argue that the shortage of women in China

ought to give them the upper hand in the marriage market. Yet patriarchal norms are still deeply entrenched throughout Chinese society. And urban, educated women who are beginning to reject these discriminatory norms are bombarded daily with media reports about how they had better stop focusing on their careers or they will never be able to find a husband.

Although some women may marry for money, I have found very little evidence that urban women overall have turned their scarcity into economic gain. On the contrary, my research suggests that Chinese women have largely missed out on what is arguably the biggest accumulation of residential real-estate wealth in history, valued at around 3.3 times China's GDP, according to figures from the bank HSBC. That amounted to over US$30 trillion at the end of 2013. Many women have been shut out of China's explosion of housing wealth because urban homes appreciating exponentially in value tend to be registered solely in the man's name. Chinese parents tend to buy homes for sons but not daughters. And women often transfer all of their assets to their husband or boyfriend to finance the purchase of a home registered in the man's name alone.

Many scholars focus on income as the primary indicator of a woman's socioeconomic status, but I argue that when analyzing economic inequality in China, it is more important to focus on wealth in the form of residential property. Chinese consumers have very few places to invest their money, so most people invest it in a home, which is the most valuable family asset and worth much more than income alone. In fact, my interest in real-estate wealth and gender began with a desire to find out why urban Chinese consumers are so obsessed with buying residential property, in spite of the fact that homes in cities such as Beijing and Shanghai are by some measures among the most expensive in the world.

Yet the more interviews I carried out, the more troubled I was by how many young, highly intelligent, university-educated, urban, professional women were willing to cede ownership of an enormously expensive home to their boyfriends or husbands, even when these women had contributed their entire life savings to the property purchase. Why would so many educated women in their mid- to late twenties act against their own economic interests? I was baffled for a while, until I started explicitly asking my interviewees about "leftover" women. And then I discovered that, in spite of their high level of education, many young women genuinely believe the destructive myths perpetuated by the state media. These women make excessive personal and financial compromises out of fear that they will never find a husband otherwise.

In one sense, "leftover" women do not exist. They are a category of women concocted by the government to achieve its demographic goals of promoting marriage, planning population, and maintaining social stability. The state media campaign against "leftover" women is just one of the signs that in recent years, contrary to many claims made by mainstream news organizations, women in China have experienced a dramatic rollback of rights and gains relative to men. It is in this larger sense that women have been "left over" and left behind by the ruling Communist Party in its breakneck race for economic growth at all costs.

It was not always like this. For all its failings, the early period following the establishment of the People's Republic of China was a time when overcoming traditional forms of male–female inequality was declared an important revolutionary goal. After the Communist revolution of 1949, Chairman Mao Zedong proclaimed that "women hold up half the sky." In the years after the revolution, the Communist Party publicly celebrated gender equality and sought to harness women's labor in boosting the nation's productivity with expansive initiatives such as assigning urban women jobs in the planned economy. Yet women's historic gains of the past are now being eroded in China's post-socialist reform era.

A combination of factors – skyrocketing home prices, a resurgence of traditional gender norms, legal setbacks to married women's property rights, declining labor force participation among women, and the media campaign against "leftover" women – has contributed to the fall in status and material well-being of Chinese women relative to men. That's more than 650 million women, almost one-fifth of all the women in the world.

This book is the result of two and a half years of research conducted during my Ph.D. program in Sociology at Tsinghua University in Beijing. In November 2010, I began an ethnographic study of several Beijing real-estate agencies, where I first noticed the prevalence of traditional gender norms in home buying. Then in August 2011, China's Supreme People's Court issued a stark new interpretation of the country's Marriage Law, reversing a cornerstone of the Communist Revolution. The Marriage Law of 1950 granted women rights to property, divorce and freedom of choice in marriage, among other rights. Subsequent revisions of the law over the years have also strengthened the notion of common marital property. Yet the Supreme Court's latest interpretation in 2011 specifies that, unless legally contested, marital property essentially belongs to the person who owns the home and whose name is on the property deed. And in China today that person is usually a man. According to a 2012 survey by Horizon China and iFeng.com of home buying in China's top real-estate markets – the cities of Beijing, Shanghai, Guangzhou, and Shenzhen – only 30 percent of marital home deeds include the woman's name, even though over 70 percent of women contribute to the marital home purchase. These figures already demonstrate an alarming disparity between property ownership by men versus women, but my research suggests that the inequality is even more extreme when considering the number of homes owned *solely* by men. Defenders of the 2011 judicial interpretation of the Marriage Law argue that women are entitled to compensation for their share of the home payments, but most women do not keep receipts of their contributions. And stay-at-home mothers have even less financial protection in the event of a divorce.

Curious about the effects of the revised Marriage Law on urban women and men, I set up a Sina Weibo account (China's version of Twitter) shortly after the legal change was announced, and called for people to take part in my study on how gender norms affect home buying. I crafted questions about the participant's identity, home-buying aspirations, and how financial contributions were divided, and sent these to everyone who expressed interest. I promised anonymity for everyone who responded to my online survey. Within days of setting up my account, over 950 men and women across China had signed up to "follow" my account publicly, and I had received around 150 private messages. I asked follow-up questions of roughly 100 people, which resulted in many extended, online interviews. My final survey results included a sample of 283 people (151 women and 132 men) from cities across China, including Beijing, Shanghai, Xi'an, Guangzhou, Shenzhen, Xiamen, Chengdu, Chongqing, Dalian, Fuzhou, Hangzhou, Suzhou, Kunming, Nanjing, Shenyang, Tianjin, Wuhan, Wenzhou, and Hohhot.

In addition to my Weibo survey, I conducted formal, in-depth interviews with 60 people (36 women and 24 men): 39 in Beijing,

18 in Shanghai, and 3 in Xi'an, with some people interviewed several times. I chose Beijing and Shanghai because they are both "first-tier" cities, where residential property is most expensive, and I conducted three interviews in Xi'an to gain some insight into whether gendered home-buying dynamics would be different in a "second-tier" city, where real-estate prices are significantly lower. Most of my formal interviewees have a college-level education or above, with an average to above-average income (and could be considered "middle class"), and are in their mid-twenties through early thirties – the prime age for marriage and first-time urban home buying in China.

China is experiencing rapid urbanization, as people from rural origins moving to cities have caused a historic shift in the country's population from majority rural to majority urban. While around half of my formal interviewees are from one-child families, the other half have siblings and have moved to Beijing, Shanghai or Xi'an from a place with fewer family-planning restrictions. I included both siblings and people from only-child families to obtain information on parents' differential treatment of daughters versus sons. Almost two-thirds of China's population are not bound by one-child policy restrictions, and urban couples can also circumvent restrictions in various ways (such as paying a fine), according to research by demographer Wang Feng and his colleagues.

I also analyzed the content of multiple state media news reports, editorials and images on the Internet regarding home buying and the phenomenon of "leftover" women. I drew on casual conversations with hundreds of Chinese women and men in Beijing over three years about gender and home buying. And at the time of writing, I continue to receive messages on my Weibo account from thousands of Internet users in China commenting on "leftover" women, home buying and gender inequality.

My thinking is informed by a lifetime of visiting the People's Republic of China as the daughter of two China scholars, Beverly Hong-Fincher and John Fincher. I made my first trip to Beijing with my mother as a three-year-old in 1971, after Henry Kissinger's secret talks with Chinese Premier Zhou Enlai paved the way for US President Richard Nixon's landmark visit in 1972, which reestablished long-severed US–China relations. I continued visiting China during many childhood summers throughout the 1970s and 1980s, and I later worked as a China-based journalist for several American news organizations from the late 1990s through to 2003.

In other, wealthier parts of East Asia, such as Japan, Hong Kong, Singapore, South Korea, and Taiwan, women are increasingly delaying marriage. In mainland China, at the time of writing, studies show that almost everyone still marries by age 35. Yet China's demographic trends may be changing, particularly in large cities such as Beijing and Shanghai.

Take 26-year-old Zhang Yu, a university graduate from Changsha, Hunan province in central China, who moved to Shanghai in 2013 to escape her family and jumpstart her career. After years of being badgered by her parents to get married, Zhang had finally had enough. "I have decided never to marry or have a child," she told me.

Zhang's vow never to marry is rare in a country where educated women are constantly told by their families, friends and the state media that they will be ostracized if they do not find a husband quickly. Yet if women's rights do not improve in China, more and more women, like Zhang, may reject marriage altogether.

Zhang had been living with her parents in Hunan to save money after obtaining her college degree, and for a time fell sway to her parents' worries that she would become a "leftover" woman. But after reading feminist websites, she came to believe that the term existed to make women return to the home. She then took a risk by moving to Shanghai without a job and leaving the comforts of home for a dorm room shared with nine other roommates. Now she loves her new friends and the sense of freedom. "Men are still thinking in the old ways, but women's values have evolved. I feel very relaxed now," said Zhang, who had just received a sales job offer when I interviewed her.

Another young woman in Beijing came to the same conclusion as Zhang. "The institution of marriage basically benefits men, and when women get hurt this institution doesn't protect our rights," she told me. "The most rational choice is to stay single."

Leftover Women: The Resurgence of Gender Inequality in China will debunk the popular myth that women overall are faring well as a result of China's post-socialist market reforms. It is impossible to address all aspects of China's gender inequality in one slim volume, and I do not focus on rural women or migrant women workers without a college education. The book focuses primarily on the consequences of the state media campaign regarding "leftover" women since 2007 and the unprecedented gender inequality in wealth created by China's urban real-estate boom. Contrary to the stereotypes of single, professional women being miserable and lonely, I will show that the reality is quite the opposite: it is young women rushing into marriage too early that tend to wind up in trouble.

Chapter 1 examines how the Chinese state media campaign regarding "leftover" women is related to the government's attempts to maintain social stability in the midst of widespread discontent. It argues that the "leftover" women media campaign serves a state program to upgrade "population quality" by pressuring educated, "high quality" women to marry and have a "high quality" baby for the good of the nation.

Chapter 2 explores how intense pressure on young women to marry in order to avoid becoming "leftover" prompts many of them to give up too much bargaining power within the marriage, out of fear that they will not find another husband. This fear feeds into a related phenomenon: how Chinese women have been shut out of arguably the biggest accumulation of residential real-estate wealth in history.

Chapter 3 analyzes gender inequality within the extended family, and considers why many parents discriminate against their own daughters by buying expensive homes for their sons only. It also explores the dynamics behind emerging middle-class Chinese consumers' obsession with buying real estate and how real-estate mania has combined with government restrictions on buying property to create an unparalleled gender wealth gap.

Chapter 4 gives some historical context to the erosion of women's property rights in China's post-socialist era. It contrasts women's weak property rights today with the situation for elite women around a thousand years ago during the Song dynasty, when more property was transferred to women than at any other time in Chinese history, according to historian Bettine Birge. It also reviews the movement for women's emancipation in the Republican period and shows how the Communist revolutionary rhetoric of gender equality conflicted with the actual situation of women during the Mao years.

Chapter 5 depicts the connection between women's lack of property rights and China's rampant problem of intimate partner violence. China is not the only country with an epidemic of domestic violence, but the absence of legal protections and the role of police as enforcers of social stability in China mean that abused women often fall into further danger and retribution when they try to reach out for help from others.

Chapter 6 depicts how the authoritarian nature of China's one-party state has prevented a nationwide women's rights movement from gaining traction. It also shows how, in spite of the repression, women find ways to fight back against entrenched gender discrimination.

Might the women of China reach a point where the constant debasement and violations of their rights give rise to a sustained, political movement? It may be difficult to picture now. But in 1907, China's female revolutionary Qiu Jin wrote that "equal rights for men and women are endowed by nature; how, then, is it that you willingly live in subordination?" A few years later, Chinese women and men fighting for greater freedoms helped bring down the Qing Empire. If history is any guide, China's leaders ignore the deepening gender inequality at their peril.

ONE

China's "leftover" women

How the state stigmatizes single educated women in their late twenties

Chen Su has a bachelor's degree in economics from a top university and works as a manager at a marketing firm in Beijing. Her steady income enables her to send money several times a year to support her parents in the southern Chinese city of Guangzhou and sometimes to help out her older brother, who has trouble managing his budget. Chen was quite pleased with her accomplishments for the first few years after college graduation, but now that she has turned 26 the pressure to get married torments her.

Chen is unhappy with her boyfriend, whom she describes as "selfish and insensitive." She tries to avoid seeing him more than once a week, because she doesn't enjoy talking to him. "The conversation is mediocre," she says. "I can't speak freely with him." He doesn't bring her along when he goes out, except once in a while when a business dinner requires him to have a female companion, and then she is expected to stay quiet. He doesn't like going out with her friends either. He's jealous. They fight a lot. But he proposed marriage to her and she is inclined to say yes. Why? One of her best friends advised her that she shouldn't hold out for another partner because "there are no naturally good men." "I am almost a 'leftover' woman," says Chen. "I don't have enough courage to break it off, and I don't think I could find a better man."

Chen may not recognize it, but she has internalized the ideology of China's mass media campaign on "leftover" women, carried out since 2007. Chen has taken to heart messages such as this from a column originally posted on the official Xinhua News website in 2008, reposted the same year on the All-China Women's Federation website, then widely recycled on state media sites over the years through 2013: "Women Marrying Late Shouldn't Blindly Let 'Late' Become 'Never'". The script exhorts women to lower their standards and stop holding out for a good partner, or they will wind up lonely forever:

> In waiting for true love to appear, women squander their precious youth. The pursuit of true love has become the most important criterion…
>
> [Women] excessively pursue perfection. The problem is that many of these women are too clear-headed, they can't tolerate weaknesses in their partner, especially since more and more women seek the "three highs" – high education, high professional achievement and high income. Their standards for their careers and their partners are so high, by the time they want to marry, they discover that almost all the men who are their equal in education and age are already married.
>
> For the group of white-collar women who don't find a partner, loneliness is a common occurrence. As these unmarried women age, the feeling of loneliness gets worse and worse.

State media news reports, surveys, columns, cartoons and television shows about "leftover" women are clearly an attempt to stop urban educated women from delaying marriage any further. Most of the messages are variations on the same theme, directed at single, educated, urban women: stop working so hard at your careers; lower your sights and don't be so ambitious; don't be so picky about whom you marry. As the Xinhua News column "Do Leftover Women Really Deserve Our Sympathy?" admonishes:

> The main reason many girls become "leftover women" is that their standards for a partner are too high ... As long as girls are not too picky, finding a partner should be as easy as blowing away a speck of dust.

My research over two and a half years indicates that the state media campaign about "leftover" women has had a powerful effect on many urban Chinese women in their twenties and early thirties. The stigma surrounding "leftover" women intensifies pressure on women in their mid- to late twenties to rush into marriage with the wrong man. It undermines women's confidence and prompts many to act against their economic interests when they marry.

The All-China Women's Federation first defined the term "leftover" women (*shengnü* 剩女) in 2007 as single women older than 27, but in fact the sustained media campaign about "leftover" women has since broadened to include women who are just 25.

In 2010, a group affiliated to the Women's Federation – the Marriage and Family Research Association – carried out a nationwide survey of more than 30,000 people in thirty-one provinces, in conjunction with the Committee of Matchmaking Service Industries and the Baihe online dating website. The widely circulated, official write-up of the survey on Chinese attitudes toward love and marriage used the subheading "See What Category of 'Leftover' You Belong To."

It identified the first category as single women aged 25 to 27 years, who are called "leftover warriors," *sheng dou shi*, a play on the title of a popular martial arts film. It said these women "still have the courage to fight for a partner." The second category is 28- to 30-year-old women, or "the ones who must triumph," *bi sheng ke*, a pun on the Chinese name for Pizza Hut, which has become a popular chain restaurant throughout China. It said these women have limited opportunities for romance because their careers leave them "no time for the hunt." The third category is 31- to 35-year-old women, "Buddha of victorious battles", *dou zhan sheng fo*, a play on the name of an ancient Chinese legend, Monkey King, when he attains the status of Buddha. It said these "high-level 'leftover' women battle to survive in the cruel workplace, but are still single." The final category, 35 and older, is called the "Great Sage Equal of Heaven" or *qi tian da sheng*, another play on the Monkey King legend. It said this category of woman "has a luxury apartment, private car and a company" but nonetheless became a "leftover" woman.

Other, supposedly objective findings from the survey on "leftover" women have been recycled frequently in the Chinese media, including a Xinhua News report, "China's 'Leftover Women' Unite This Singles Day." The report states that, "more than 90 percent of men surveyed said women should marry before 27 to avoid becoming unwanted."

Why would the Women's Federation be involved in efforts to stigmatize educated single women? It was established by the Communist Party in 1949 as the feminist agency of the Chinese state, to uphold "equality between women and men" and "protect women's rights and interests." Women's liberation was a rallying cry of the Communist Revolution and cadres in the Women's Federation played a prominent role in the campaign to promoting gender equality, particularly in the countryside, where they sponsored literacy classes and other projects to improve women's social standing. Over the years, the Women's Federation has also promoted good research on the status of women in Chinese society.

Yet, despite its feminist mandate, scholars have demonstrated that the Women's Federation was in many ways not so different from any other organ of the Communist Party. When the Communist Party adopted its "one-child policy," it assigned primary responsibility for enforcing the harsh population controls to the Women's Federation, which carried out invasive monitoring of women's reproductive lives and forced women to have abortions, "permanently tarnishing its reputation as an advocacy group for women," according to historian Rebecca Karl's book *Mao Zedong and China in the Twentieth Century*. Under the Party's control, "women's bodies became mere objects of state contraceptive control, vehicles for the achievement of urgent demographic targets," according to population specialist Susan Greenhalgh. Literary critic Lydia H. Liu writes that the Women's Federation functioned "in reality very much like other hegemonic apparatuses used by the Party," while historian Tani Barlow says the Women's Federation used its power to "subordinate and dominate inscriptions of womanhood." In fact, the peculiarity of a *Women's* Federation that contributes to bolstering male supremacy is matched only by the ways that the country's official *Labor* Federation often serves more to control than to empower workers.

Perhaps it should be no surprise, then, that the Women's Federation took a key role in the campaign to compel urban educated women to stop focusing on their careers and get married. Most written reports denigrating "leftover" women have been republished almost verbatim, multiple times over the years, originally by the official Xinhua News agency, and then posted on the Women's Federation website. Take this Xinhua News column, "Eight Simple Moves to Escape the Leftover Women Trap," which urges women to "seduce but don't pester" and "be persistent but not willful":

> When holding out for a man, if you say he must be rich and
> brilliant, romantic and hard-working … this is just being willful.
> Does this kind of perfect man exist? Maybe he does exist, but why
> on earth would he want to marry you?

I decided to try to trace roughly how many times this particular column had been reposted over the years. The column was originally published by the Xinhua News website in 2007, then posted the same year on the website of the All-China Women's Federation, then reposted multiple times over the years on all of China's major portals and search engines, including sina.com, sohu.com, baidu.com, lady.qq.com, sex.39.net, pclady.com, hexun.com, blog163.com, and so on (I lost count after noting several dozen websites). Then the Xinhua News website published the same column verbatim in 2010, and it was reposted again multiple times in multiple venues, including again on the website of the Women's Federation in 2011. The last time I checked, the Xinhua News website had again reposted the same column in January 2013, except that it had changed the title slightly from "Eight Simple Moves to Escape the Leftover Women Trap" to "Eight Moves Teaching You to Speedily Escape the Leftover Women Trap." The only other alteration was that with each reposting of the column, the accompanying photographs were different.

The Women's Federation has dutifully reposted many of the Xinhua News articles about "leftover" women on its official website since 2007, including the column "Do Leftover Women Really Deserve Our Sympathy?" This one accused educated single women of sleeping around and having degenerate morals:

> Many highly educated "leftover women" are very progressive in
> their thinking and enjoy going to nightclubs in search of a one-
> night stand, or they become the mistress of a high official or rich

man. It is only when they have lost their youth and are kicked out by the man that they decide to look for a life partner. Therefore most "leftover women" do not deserve our sympathy.

And once a woman finds marital bliss, what should she do if her husband has an affair? Consider this Xinhua News editorial, reposted on the Women's Federation website (and multiple other venues) under the headline "Faced with a Marital Crisis, Women Need to Improve Themselves":

> When you find out that he is having an affair, you may be in a towering rage, but you must know that if you make a fuss, you are denying the man "face" … No man is capable of spending a lifetime being loyal to an outmoded wife who never changes … Try changing your hairstyle or your fashion. Women must constantly change for the better.

In other words, according to the state media, married women's husbands only have affairs because their wives are too dull, and "leftover" women are only single because they are too picky. It is worth noting that none of the state media editorials warns men to be more caring husbands or their wives will start having affairs.

Marriage, social stability and upgrading "population quality"

Despite the media frenzy over "leftover" women who are supposedly doomed to stay single forever, China actually faces a *shortage* of marriage-age women. The country's sex ratio imbalance has created a demographic crisis of tens of millions of surplus or "leftover" men (*shengnan*), who will be unable to find a bride. In general, the normal ratio of boys to girls at birth is recognized to be around 105 to 100. Yet many factors – including China's one-child policy, a traditional preference for boys, access to technology that allows parents to detect the sex of their fetus, and resultant sex-selective abortions – have caused the country's sex ratio imbalance to rise steadily until its peak of roughly 121 boys to 100 girls in 2008, according to Xinhua News. It has now fallen slightly to 117.7 boys to 100 girls in 2012, but at the time of writing China's sex ratio imbalance at birth is one of the highest ever observed in the world. (Other countries with a high ratio of boys to girls caused by sex selection include India, with around 110 boys to 100 girls; Pakistan, 109 to 100; Azerbaijan, 116 to 100; Armenia, 114 to 100; Albania, 111 to 100; and Vietnam, 111 boys to 100 girls, according to figures from the United Nations Population Fund.)

China's crisis of millions of men unable to find wives is not merely a problem for the future; it is already happening within the prime marrying-age population, according to the National Bureau of Statistics (NBS). In June, 2012, an editorial in the *People's Daily* – the mouthpiece of the Chinese Communist Party – warned of potentially grave demographic dangers ahead:

> The sex ratio imbalance will affect the future development of our population. Since women are those directly giving birth, the deficit in women will inevitably lead to a decline in the birth rate, which will further reduce the total population and the scale of the working-age population and speed up aging of the population... In the long run, the inability of "surplus" men to have a spouse and child poses the problem of how they will take care of themselves and their parents in the future. ... The continual accumulation of unmarried men of legal marrying age greatly increases the risk of social instability and insecurity. This report says that older unmarried men in villages surveyed in the past three years have taken part in activities destroying social order, including gambling, rioting, stealing and gang fighting.

News reports and studies abound that focus on the wretched lives of millions of surplus men, known as "bare branches" (*guanggun*) for their male appendages and inability to produce an heir. Most of these men are poor, uneducated and rural. Mara Hvistendahl writes in her book on the global sex ratio imbalance, *Unnatural Selection*, about some remote parts of China with villages teeming with men, where the ratio of boys to girls had reached 3 to 2. The state media do not blame these men for being single, however. The matchmaking website Jiayuan.com conducted a study in 2013 on "leftover" men, focusing on survey respondents between 29 and 39 years old. While it found that "leftover" men are more likely to be uneducated and poor than "leftover" women, it also found that in stark contrast to educated single women, educated men are generally in no rush to marry: "Even though the wolves are many and the meat is little [*lang duo rou shao*] ... the vast majority of single men over 30 consider themselves to be in their golden years, without the slightest bit of pressure [to marry]." Here, "wolves" stand for men, while "meat" refers to women.

As one popular Chinese saying goes, *nanren sanshi yi duo hua, nüren sanshi lan zhazha*, meaning "men of 30 are like a flower, women at 30 are wilted and rotten." The rhyme and richness of the Chinese verse is lost in translation, but the double standard regarding single men as compared with women could not be more obvious. Chinese men continue to enjoy a privileged position in society in spite of the sex ratio imbalance. It is easy to see the rationale for a campaign playing on the natural insecurities of single *women* instead, to pressure them to marry some of the millions of actually existing "leftover" men.

Restless single men are seen as a threat to the foundation of Chinese society. And single women threaten the moral fabric as well, for being free agents, unnatural in failing to perform their duty to give birth to a child and tame a restless man. From the government's perspective, married couples are much less likely to cause trouble. As any Communist Party publication will tell you, marriage and family form "the basic cell of society" and "a harmonious family is the foundation of a harmonious society." China's president from 2003 to 2013, Hu Jintao, coined the term "harmonious society" to describe the ideal socialist society, where social stability and order prevail.

Yet, in the face of widespread inequality and social discontent, the goal of the "harmonious society" (*hexie shehui*) has justified the means of "maintaining stability" (*weiwen*) at all costs. Tsinghua University sociologists in Beijing released a report in 2010, detailing the ways in which the Chinese state's obsession with maintaining stability caused a vicious cycle of instability and conflict. One of the report's authors, Professor Sun Liping, estimated that in 2010 China had 180,000 protests or "mass incidents." For three consecutive years since then, China's internal security budget has exceeded the budget for national defense, indicating the government's continuing fears about domestic threats. In 2013, the Chinese government's publicly declared defense budget was RMB 740.6 billion (US$119 billion), compared with RMB 769.1 billion (US$124 billion) for domestic security, covering police, state security, armed civil militia, courts and jails. There are "hard" measures to maintain stability, through arrests, threats and intimidation of protesters and dissidents. But equally important in protecting the social order are the "soft" ideological measures for the general public, such as education, media campaigns to promote marriage, and government-sponsored matchmaking.

One startling example of how the Communist Party promotes marriage for social stability occurred in the aftermath of the devastating 2008 Sichuan earthquake, which resulted in 87,000 dead or missing and almost 400,000 injured. Brook Larmer reports in the *New York Times* how Chinese government officials mobilized widows and widowers in Beichuan, a town almost completely leveled by the earthquake, to marry each other: "How can society rebuild? In China, one answer has been to pair grieving men and women to create instant families that will help ensure social and economic stability." Thanks to the marriage mobilization drive, less than eight months after the earthquake, 614 survivors had already remarried, many of them to each other out of "patriotic duty," according to the *Times*. In a more recent example of attempted marriage promotion, in June 2013 the city of Wuhan proposed a draft regulation to fine single mothers. Women who have a child out of wedlock would be fined around RMB 82,000 (US$13,000), or about four times the average annual income in Wuhan, although Wuhan reportedly watered down the plan after an outcry.

China's state media campaign regarding "leftover" women is part of an overall effort to promote marriage for social stability. News outlets have deployed the different categories of "leftover" women in a multitude of cartoons or staged photographs accompanying their reports. These illustrations are mostly variations on the same visual themes: the woman is highly educated, successful, and perched high above the men beneath her (an oblique reference to China's demographic surplus of men), whom she has presumably rejected in her blind pursuit of her career goals. Some of the illustrations include images of anguished parents looking on in disappointment at their unmarried daughters.

The fact that state media portrayals of "leftover" women almost always show them to be "highly educated" demonstrates the great progress made by urban women in education over the past decade or more. Almost 26 percent of urban women in China received a college-level education or higher in 2010 – an increase of 13 percentage points compared with a decade ago, according to the Third Survey on the Social Status of Women, carried out by the NBS and the Women's Federation. The survey indicates that many women are outperforming men at university, with around 62 percent of university-level women showing "excellent academic performance," compared with 53 percent of their male classmates. Women now outnumber men in undergraduate and master's programs, according to the Ministry of Education. Record numbers of women in China are also taking the GMAT entrance test for business schools worldwide (although some women tell me they are anxious to leave China precisely because they face so much gender discrimination at home).

Yet the state media "leftover" women narrative takes this tremendous accomplishment of urban Chinese women and turns it into an object of mockery. The image of the educated woman, supposedly too smart and intimidating to attract a husband, appears repeatedly in cartoon images. One popular cartoon shows a woman with a birthday cake showing the giant number "27" in melting candles. The woman – who is wearing thick-rimmed glasses to indicate her high education – contorts her face in frustration and stands behind the giant "27" on the cake, with cobwebs attached to her and objects like a notebook and pen flying chaotically around her. Outside, snow gathers heavily on her roof, while the smoke above her chimney forms the character *jiong*, a new word whose meaning – "depressed" or "frustrated" – is embodied in its form, shaped like an upset face. The woman appears much like a younger version of Charles Dickens's famous "spinster" Miss Havisham of the novel *Great Expectations*, with a caption above her saying: "I don't even feel like I've grown up yet, but I wasn't careful, so I've become conspicuously 'leftover'."

A twist on the theme shows a woman shivering in her graduation gown, mortarboard on her head, clutching her university diploma as she stands on top of a tower covered with snow, with a blizzard of snowflakes swirling around her. Her eyes are bulging from fright or cold, and the caption on her tower reads: "Urban 'Leftover' Woman Seeks Marriage Partner." The poor frigid woman is out of luck as the two men standing beneath her tower reject her. In contrast to the cold blizzard battering the woman on the tower, there is no snowstorm where the two men are standing, and they appear to be very comfortable and warm in their coats, scarves, hats and gloves. "She's too highly educated," says one man. "She's too successful," says the other.

Another widely circulated cartoon shows a young woman wearing thick-rimmed glasses (indicating her university education) peering out from behind the parapet of a tall castle. The caption above her head reads: "Why hasn't my Prince Charming appeared with his white horse? If I keep waiting, this Snow White will turn into an old witch!" The tower beneath her is emblazoned with three bold captions, reading: "High Education, High [Professional] Position, High Income." At the base of the cartoon are blurry images of masses of heads, representing the millions of surplus men in China. An alternate version of this theme shows three women standing on a high platform, blind to the masses of men gathered below. Two of the women are peering off into the distance through their binoculars, while one woman has cupped her eyes with her hands and is staring at the sky above her, implicitly looking for a dream husband while ignoring the real men below. The platform on which the women stand has three blocks, again reading: "High Education, High [Professional] Position, High Income."

A different cartoon theme shows a woman wearing a white bridal gown with a mortarboard on her head indicating her university education, as she stands beneath the sign for Double Happiness, symbolizing marriage. But instead of a man standing next to her, the bride is holding up a man's empty suit on a coat hanger, with a pair of shoes on the floor: she wants to be a bride but can't find anyone to marry her. In another version, the woman in the bridal gown and thick-rimmed glasses wearing a mortarboard is running frantically – sweat pouring down her face, sloppy jeans and sneakers showing beneath her wedding gown – as she chases a winged cupid with a bow. The entire picture is framed by red rose petals shaped in the form of a heart. In a photographic version of this theme, the woman is looking directly at the viewer with her arms around a man with his back to us. His head and most of his body are obscured by a giant question mark, and the caption above the photo reads: "'Leftover' Women – Persevere or Compromise?" That is, women of the "leftover" age could persevere in waiting for the perfect man, or they could make the wiser choice to compromise and marry someone who isn't perfect, but is real.

Some of the illustrations play on the words *shengnü* for "leftover" women, but use a homonym for the word *sheng*, meaning "saint" or "holy." One popular cartoon shows a woman wearing a crown inscribed with the characters *shengnü* (剩女), "saintly woman," implying that the woman is a virgin who has never had any men in her life. In addition to the crown, she also has an award ribbon draped across her chest, displaying the phrase "Great Sage Equal of Heaven" or *qi tian da sheng*, the last official category for "leftover" women aged 35 and older. Beside the woman, the bloodied and battered sword she has used to slay men is stuck in the ground. Blood from her sword drips down all three platforms beneath her chair, and at the bottom of the platforms lies a pile of the bloody corpses of men, one trampled bouquet of roses, and one discarded sign saying "love." Each platform is inscribed with one subcategory of "leftover" women: "Buddha of Victorious Battles" or *dou zhan sheng fo* for women aged 31 to 35; "The Ones Who Must Triumph" or *bi sheng ke*, women aged 28 to 30; and at the bottom, "Leftover Warriors" or *sheng doushi*, women aged 25 to 27. The implication is that this woman had to fight brutally in order to reach the pinnacle of success, but will spend the rest of her life sexless and alone. One cartoon simply shows a skeleton dressed in women's clothing, gathering cobwebs on a park bench, accompanied by the caption "still waiting for the perfect man."

Marriage promotion for social stability is one factor behind the "leftover" women media campaign. Another is related to the Chinese government's population planning goals. I believe it is no coincidence that the Women's Federation website posted its first article on "leftover" women in 2007, shortly after China's State Council – the country's Cabinet – issued its "Decision on Fully Enhancing the Population and Family Planning Program and Comprehensively Addressing Population Issues" to address "unprecedented population pressures." The State Council names the sex-ratio imbalance as one of the population pressures because it "causes a threat to social stability." It also cites the "low quality of the general population, which makes it hard to meet the requirements of fierce competition for national strength." The State Council names "upgrading population quality (*suzhi*)" as one of its key goals, and appoints the Women's Federation as one of the primary implementers of its population planning policy, along with other agencies such as Propaganda, Public Security and Civil Affairs.

The notion of cultivating "quality" citizens as a developmental goal is not as controversial in China as it is in many other countries. Many scholars have analyzed the importance of population quality or *suzhi* in Chinese government policy. Anthropologist Ellen Judd wrote in her book *The Chinese Women's Movement between State and Market* about how the term *suzhi* took on particular significance within the Women's Federation and other government initiatives to improve women's education and development. Moreover, China's population planning policy was designed to control not just the quantity of people in the country, but also the quality. As cultural studies expert Professor Harriet Evans points out, in 1995 China introduced the Law on Maternal and Infant Health Care, previously named the "Draft Eugenics Law." "Only in exceptional cases of 'mental or contagious disease' is it considered legitimate – indeed given the full backing of a eugenics law – for women 'to defer marriage' and not to have children," writes Evans.

Demographers Susan Greenhalgh and Edwin W. Winckler write that the state has in recent years moved away from aggressive and coercive family planning, such as forced abortions (although these still happen) to influencing the public through educational campaigns. They describe how the goal is to create "neoliberal subjects" who govern themselves in accordance with the priorities of the state. Greenhalgh elaborates on the role of eugenics in China's population planning policy in her book *Cultivating Global Citizens: Population in the Rise of China*:

The eugenics campaign – *yousheng youyu*, literally superior birth and child rearing – incorporated genetic engineering, but it was much broader than that, reflecting the view that humans are shaped by a broad array of genetic, environmental and educational factors, most of which can be nurtured so that human potential can be molded to meet the nation's needs.

What better way to upgrade the quality of the population than to convince educated "high-quality" women to marry and have a child for the good of the nation? The very people the Chinese government would like to see having babies are highly educated urban women, who would be able to produce children with "superior" genetic make-up, and provide these children with the most nurturing environment possible.

As women's education improves and they have the opportunity to achieve more in their careers, they naturally want to delay marriage. The mean age at first marriage among women and men in mainland China has increased slightly in recent years: it was around 25 for women and 27 for men according to the 2010 census, up from around 23 for women and 25 for men in 2000. But in neighboring Japan, Taiwan, Singapore, South Korea and Hong Kong, the marriage age has risen much more sharply than in China, and increasing numbers of educated women do not marry at all. If Chinese women were to follow their sisters in neighboring regions and reject marriage as well, it would deal a devastating blow to the Chinese government's population planning goals.

Since 2008, local population planning commissions in cities such as Nanjing and Ningbo have carried out "interventions" to resolve the perceived "crisis" of growing numbers of women remaining single. One article in the *Jinling* [Nanjing] *Evening Post* ran the headline "Nanjing 'Urban Leftover Women' Phenomenon Worsens by the Day – Population Planning Committee Plans

Intervention." Local Women's Federation branches have arranged matchmaking events for "highly educated, high-quality" women, such as an initiative in Pinghu, Zhejiang Province, in March 2012, for "leftover women to speedily find conjugal happiness." Since 2011, various divisions of the Shanghai government – including the Shanghai Women's Federation, Shanghai Civil Affairs Bureau, and the government-affiliated Shanghai Matchmaking Agency Management Association – have collaborated to organize mass matchmaking fairs for educated women and men. Almost 40,000 young women and men registered for the 2013 and 2012 fairs, more than 80 percent of whom had undergraduate degrees or higher, according to the official Xinhua News Agency.

Xinhua News ran a report with the advertisement-like headline "This Year's Mass Matchmaking Fair – 30 percent of Women Are in the 'Post-'90' Generation [born after 1990] – Register before this Friday." Xinhua reported that the youngest woman at the 2013 Shanghai matchmaking fair was just 21 years old. Several media outlets quote her as saying, "next year I will be considered of 'late marriage' age, so in order to avoid becoming a 'leftover' woman like the earlier generation, it's better to join the matchmaking groups ahead of schedule." The 21-year-old woman's name is not provided in the news reports, so it is entirely possible that her statement was made up for propaganda purposes. Shanghai's matchmaking fairs have become so popular that Shanghai will start holding two mass fairs a year starting in the second half of 2013. The Shanghai Matchmaking Agency Management Association has also started to schedule monthly matchmaking events for a more "intimate" number of urban residents, limited to just 300 a time. Moreover, government-sponsored, mass matchmaking fairs are also spreading to other large cities such as Hangzhou, the capital of eastern Zhejiang province, where a fair in November 2013 attracted around 50,000 people (including parents of the young women and men), according to Xinhua.

Another aspect of China's effort to upgrade population quality is the state media's regular reports on babies born with birth defects, attributed in large part to "women having their first child at an older age." The official *People's Daily* website ran a report in September 2013 under the headline "Numbers Show that Beijing Has Over 4000 Children with Birth Defects Each Year, Cases Rise in Recent Years." The opening sentence of the article issues this warning: "Due to the increasing proportion of older women giving birth over the years, and other social factors, statistics show that Beijing's rates of birth defects have risen in recent years."

A related report by the official Xinhua News Agency in September 2012 says that more than 900,000 babies are born with birth defects in China each year, citing Ministry of Health statistics. The Xinhua News report refers to unnamed experts who say the increase in birth defects is linked to the withdrawal of compulsory premarital health exams in 2003 and rising numbers of women having their first child "at an older age." The state media generally make little or no mention of scientific studies indicating that China's rise in birth defects is related to extreme levels of pollution, especially in areas of the country that are heavily reliant on coal-fired power plants. Scientists Aiguo Ren, Xinghua Qiu, Lei Jin and colleagues published a study in the Proceedings of the National Academy of Sciences in 2011 which examined the alarmingly high rates of infants born with neural tube defects in Shanxi province, a center for China's coal industry. The study found that the placentas of infants with the birth defects contained unusually high levels of "persistent organic pollutants" such as polycyclic aromatic hydrocarbons (PAHs), which are released into the air when coal and other fossil fuels are burned.

Rather than focus on the extraordinary degradation of China's environment, however, state media reports on birth defects effectively blame women for choosing to delay marriage and childbirth, or for failing to have premarital medical examinations. Susan Greenhalgh analyzes the official narrative surrounding birth defects in her book *Cultivating Global Citizens*:

> The rise in birth defects not only burdens families and society at large, the official story claims, it undermines the project of creating a biologically optimal population and of improving human capital more generally. As a top population official put it, this trend "directly affects China's comprehensive national strength, its international competitiveness, [and] sustainable socioeconomic development, as well as the realization of our strategic vision to construct a full-scale well-off society." The solution – now a major priority – is to proactively prevent birth defects by various means of genetic "engineering" that involve upgrading women's health services and universalizing prenatal genetic screening, counseling and diagnosis.

Yet the state rhetoric on preventing birth defects through promoting earlier marriage and premarital health screening – as opposed to scientific reporting on the ill effects of pollution – strikes fear in the hearts of Chinese women in their twenties who hope one day to have a child.

Women from across China have sent messages to my Weibo account, expressing their frustrations regarding the pressure to have a child while they are still in their twenties. "The government and state media keep spreading the idea that children born to women older than thirty will be bad… This just makes pregnant women deeply worried and sick at heart," wrote one woman from Shaoxing, Zhejiang province. A woman from Wuhan wrote:

"My father says that after age 30 I won't be able to have any children at all." Her comment was followed by repeated icons of angry, red faces.

Many of the women I interviewed in Beijing and Shanghai say they have been warned by their doctor during routine physical check-ups (or, in a couple of cases, by their biology professor) that they risk having a baby with birth defects if they wait until they are 28 or 30 to have a child. They fear not just the label of "leftover" woman, but the prospect of passing their "best childbearing years" if they do not marry by their late twenties.

Considering all the other signs of the Communist Party's retreat from gender equality, the media campaign regarding "leftover" women appears to be part of a backlash against women's gains of the recent past. China's post-socialist reforms since the late 1980s have led to a sweeping expansion of educational opportunities for women, making young, urban women today arguably the most highly educated in Chinese history. The increased educational opportunities of urban women led many scholars a decade ago to refer to trends such as a general "empowerment of urban daughters" under China's one-child policy, which meant that urban women generally no longer had to compete with brothers for parental investment in education. However, I believe that expectations about women's empowerment in post-socialist China have proven to be overly optimistic.

If intense pressure to marry isn't enough to deter women from pursuing higher education, the Ministry of Education has introduced gender-based quotas favoring men in college entrance exams for certain programs. In just one example in 2012, Beijing's China University of Political Science and Law required women to score 632 points to gain entrance to sciences courses, whereas men only needed 588 points, according to the *New York Times*'s

Didi Kirsten Tatlow. An official at the university told the *Times* that higher requirements for women in criminology courses were justified: "Female students must account for less than 15 percent of students because of the nature of their future career." The Ministry of Education introduced the higher barriers for women after figures showed increasing enrolment and better test results for women relative to men. For example, women made up 50.3 percent of master's degree students in 2010, up from 44.1 percent in 2004, according to the *21st Century Business Herald*.

Once a Chinese woman succeeds in going to college and has the resourcefulness to make it past the gender-based quotas to graduate from a master's degree program as well, by the time she graduates she is likely to be around 25 years old. According to the official Xinhua News Agency, women aged 25 to 27 fall within the first category of "leftover warriors" who "still have the courage to fight to find a partner."

Dismantling women's gains of the past

In recent years, a stream of rosy media accounts in the international press has told the world to look to China as a model of gender equality in the workplace. "China Dominates List of Female Billionaires," "Women in China: the Sky's the Limit," and "China the Promised Land for Women in Senior Management" are just a small sampling of the headlines. Yet the cascade of optimistic portraits detracts from what is really happening to women in China's urbanizing workforce. The fact is, they are losing ground fast.

China's gender income gap has increased substantially in the last twenty years. In 1990 the average annual salary of an urban woman was 77.5 percent that of men. But by 2010 the gap relative to men had widened by 10.2 percentage points, with urban women's average income just 67.3 percent that of men, according to demographer Isabelle Attané's analysis of figures from the All-China Women's Federation and NBS. (Rural women fare even worse relative to men, making on average just 56 percent of men's annual income.)

Urban women are also increasingly dropping out of the workforce. China's 2010 census put the percentage of women aged 20 to 59 in the labor force at 73.6 percent. The figure stacks up well against other countries such as the United States and Australia, where the 2010 labor force participation rate for women aged 25 to 54 was 75.2 percent, according to a National Bureau of Economic Research paper by economists Francine Blau and Lawrence Kahn. Female labor force participation in Sweden was 87.5 percent, in France 83.8 percent, and in the United Kingdom 78.7 percent, according to Blau and Kahn's analysis of Organization for Economic Cooperation and Development employment figures for 2010.

Yet China's figure for female labor force participation is high because it includes women working in the countryside; unlike in developed countries, nearly half of China's population is still rural. The picture for *urban* women is very different. China's urban employment rate for women aged 20 to 59 fell to a new low of 60.8 percent in 2010, down from 77.4 percent twenty years earlier, according to census figures. The 2010 rate was 20.3 percentage points lower than that of men, whereas in 1990 urban women's employment rate was 14.5 percentage points lower than that of men. That is, while gender gaps in employment are narrowing throughout much of the world, China's gender gap has *widened* significantly over the past two decades.

This widening gender gap in urban employment and income

matters because the effort to move people from the countryside to the cities is a top policy priority of China's new leaders — one that they see as crucial to boosting economic growth. China's urbanization rate was expected to rise to 53.37 percent in 2013, and Chinese state media say that 60 percent of China's population of nearly 1.4 billion will likely be urban by 2020. Yet the presumed economic benefits of urbanization cannot be realized if the talents of half the country's population – women – are squandered in the process.

The decline in urban women's labor participation looks even worse if you go further back, to the end of the 1970s, when over 90 percent of working-age women in the cities were employed, according to sociologist Jiang Yongping. That resulted from the Communist Party's mass mobilization of its people to bolster the nation's productivity and its declared commitment to gender equality. But the state-imposed equal employment of women and men failed to transform underlying gender relations. Behind the public celebration of gender equality in the Communist workplace, women continued to shoulder the heavy burdens of childcare, housework and cooking at home.

Urban women's employment rates started to drop precipitously when China fired tens of millions of workers at state-owned enterprises (SOEs) in the 1990s as part of a reorganization of the national economy. Women were fired disproportionately over men, and women were rehired later at much lower rates than men who were fired, according to sociologist Liu Jieyu's book *Gender and Work in Urban China*. The fall in labor force participation was particularly sharp among women older than 45 in the 1990s, according to sociologist Liu Jingming's analysis of China's labor market. This trend was exacerbated by the 1978 State Council regulation mandating that women who are ordinary workers must retire at age 50, while men may retire at age 60.

A "Women Return to the Home" movement emerged in the 1990s, calling on women to quit their jobs to make way for men in a time of rising unemployment, sociologist Tong Xin explains in a paper on Chinese gender studies. Over the years, these attitudes have taken hold: there has been a resurgence of belief in traditional gender roles. Most Chinese men and women still believe in the notion that men belong outside (in public), women belong inside (at home). The number of men and women who believe in this traditional gender division has increased by eight percentage points and four percentage points respectively over the past decade – to 61.6 percent of men and 54.8 percent of women – according to a 2010 survey by the All-China Women's Federation and NBS.

Gender discrimination in hiring has become rampant as China's economy is increasingly dominated by the services sector. Service employers explicitly advertise for women who are young, beautiful and "feminine," according to sociologist Eileen Otis's book *Markets and Bodies: Women, Service Work and the Making of Inequality in China*:

> Characteristics of the body (age, sex, height, weight, skin tone, comportment) are now a basis for the segmentation of labor markets and also determine the length of a woman's occupational lifetime in services. Service employers routinely dismiss workers as they approach their late twenties, when their physical beauty is thought to be diminished. To describe this state of affairs, working-class women invoke a subsistence metaphor, calling service work a "spring rice bowl" (*qingchunfanwan*).

Employment discrimination against women is by no means confined to those in the working class. One university-educated advertising art director I interviewed in Beijing was successful in her field until she had a child at the age of 33. She thought she could afford to leave her job for a couple of years to look after her baby without hurting her career. She was wrong. Now 37 years old, she has had no luck getting rehired. "I am very worried about my future because it is so difficult for a woman of my age to find work," she says.

To make matters worse, the state media campaign regarding "leftover" women has prompted some highly educated women to quit their jobs even before they get married, out of fear that they might become "too old" to find a husband. One young, university-educated Beijinger I met wanted to make herself a more attractive marriage candidate, less intimidating to suitors. "My most important duty is to find a good man to marry," she said. How did she fulfill that duty? By dropping out of the workforce.

During the early years of the People's Republic, by contrast, the systematic assignment of jobs to urban residents meant that dropping out of the workforce was not an option for the vast majority of women. Although women in the planned economy had to assume a double burden of working in the paid labor force as well as at home, historian Wang Zheng writes that

> in the Mao era, employment was taken for granted as an important component of a woman's life… Women's employment enhanced their status at home since their income was vitally important to the family in the egalitarian low-income system of the Mao era.

After years of the relentless barrage of misogynistic state media reports, some Chinese women are pushing back against the sexist nature of the "leftover" women term through social media. Consider just a tiny sample of the many comments posted to my Weibo account from women throughout China:

> The *shengnü* ["leftover" women] ideology is a rape of the hearts and minds of China's women! China is a male chauvinist society through and through, but Chinese men are still not satisfied.
>
> Can't women have the right to choose our own way of life? Why must a woman who chooses to be single be vilified by all of society?
>
> Boycott! Marriage is over! Much better to buy yourself a home, get somebody's sperm, and raise a child, rather than wait on a man!
>
> Sisters, public opinion is very powerful, but don't let it brainwash you… Don't be afraid to be single.

Some women say they are subverting the term *shengnü*, using it "as a marker of pride rather than shame, just like the term *queer* in English has been reclaimed." One declared: "I'm 'leftover' and proud of it!"

Women have created positive new sayings by using homonyms for the term *sheng*, turning the meaning from "leftover" (剩) to "triumphant" (胜), such as this catchy phrase posted to my account: "*you shengnü, lie shengnan*" or "superior, triumphant women versus inferior, leftover men" (which sounds and rhymes much better in Chinese).

In December 2012, a woman tweeted on Weibo the Chinese translation of a *New York Times* op-ed I wrote, which criticized the Women's Federation's propagation of the term "leftover" women. She attached the following comment to my op-ed: "More and more, I believe in the saying, 'the Women's Federation is an evil organization'." Her comment (along with my op-ed) was re-tweeted many hundreds of times, until the Women's Federation website suddenly – with no explanation or apology – deleted many of its columns stigmatizing "leftover" women. This marked a minor victory for feminist activists on social media, and at the time I was hopeful that the "leftover" women media campaign might be coming to an end.

Yet, throughout 2013, the state media continued to stigmatize single women and promote an ideal of the docile wife. The Communist Party flagship publication, the *People's Daily*, featured a special Internet slide show on "leftover" women in August 2013. The accompanying text says: "Single, highly educated and well-paid as they may be, they are the ones who are left behind. In this time of desperation, in what way are Chinese women struggling for love?" The photos include one young woman auditioning for a blind date contest by packing a man's suitcase, carefully folding his trousers and shirts in one compartment, books and pens in another, while a marriage counselor looks on. The caption says: "She received positive comments from the marriage counselor due to her neat and orderly arrangement."

Moreover, China's National Population and Family Planning Commission created a new myth of *dashu kong*, or "older man obsession" in its 2012–13 survey on love and marriage. The survey, sponsored by China's biggest matchmaking website, Jiayuan.com, claims that "70 percent of women aged 18–25 years crave men 10 years older." Shortly after the survey came out in early 2013, I received dozens of messages on my Weibo account complaining about media distortions of young Chinese women's "obsession" with older men. One woman wrote that her husband told her: "'This survey says most young girls like much older men,' then he narrowed his eyes and said, 'you're too old to be my partner.'" She inserted the symbol of a person crying and wrote, "overly confident older men can only resort to violence." Again, it may not be a coincidence that the media campaign about the "older man obsession" came out at the same time that the government released new statistics showing that the ratio of single men to single women is greatest for people born between 1970 and 1980, who are now between 33 and 43 years old. The *People's Daily* says that there are 206 single men for every 100 single women in this age group. So perhaps marrying off young women with much older men might be just the solution.

The Chinese state media respond to social changes by constantly inventing new ways to insult single women, and finding new groups of women to fit within the "leftover" category. The Xinhua News website ran a column in November 2013 with the headline "Eight Kinds of Women Easily Become Leftover – One Look and Men Want to Run Away." Xinhua has published variations of this column since 2007, blaming women who are afraid of love, women who don't like sex, women who are overly focused on their careers and so forth. But on this occasion, Xinhua reflected the reality of sharply rising divorce rates in China by adding divorced, single mothers to the "leftover" category:

> She uses her children as an excuse, but in reality she is rejecting commitment and fears love… Being a mother is an excuse for her to evade her responsibilities to her basic, womanly needs. However, when the children are grown and need to leave home, they may experience a very serious sense of guilt because their mother remained single for their sake, she gave up her own happiness, and this is a sacrifice.

(Interestingly, the Xinhua News column refers to "children" rather than "child", an admission that the state's one-child policy is being whittled away.)

The Xinhua News website also ran a column in April 2013 with the headline "'Female Ph.D.s' and 'Leftover Women Home Owners'." The column describes a new trend of single women buying homes of their own in an attempt to achieve economic security, and concludes that such women are unlikely ever to find a husband. It quotes a man commenting on a single woman who has just bought a home:

> Now that you own a home, your personal worth has increased by at least 2 million [RMB]. So you must look for a man who is worth at least 2 million as well. But I hear that these kinds of men, if they are not already married, have already been married many times before. So the odds against your ever getting married have just increased to the nth degree.

The column then says that single female homeowners are the equivalent of women with Ph.D.s, who are the butt of a long-running joke that there are three genders in China: men, women, and women with Ph.D.s. The joke implies that men marry women, but women with Ph.D.s don't marry. Now, according to the Xinhua News column, single women with homes don't marry either.

Meanwhile, the damage from the "leftover" women media campaign has already been done. It has intensified pressure on educated young women to marry and have a child before time runs out for them. This pressure on women to avoid becoming "leftover" results in extremely damaging economic consequences when they marry and feeds into the phenomenon explored in Chapter 2: why many Chinese women have been shut out of what is arguably the biggest accumulation of residential real-estate wealth in history, valued at over US$30 trillion in 2013.

TWO

How Chinese women were shut out of the biggest accumulation of real-estate wealth in history

On the face of it, Wu Mei represents the modern Chinese woman who has achieved spectacular success. Just 31 years old, she makes around RMB 1 million (almost US$160,000 in 2012) a year as an attorney in Beijing, a salary that places her in the top 1 percent income bracket in China. Slender and beautiful, she could be the perfect cover model for, say, a magazine feature on "China's richest women." Yet as she speaks, a darker picture emerges. Wu recently managed to gain a divorce from an abusive husband after five years of marriage, but only by giving up her home, her life savings, and most of her other belongings.

"I cried every day on my drive home from work. I just wanted to escape," says Wu, her eyes welling with tears as she recalls the violence of her married life.

Wu's top university scores had secured her admission to a prestigious law school in Australia. Shortly after she graduated and returned to Beijing at age 25, she married an acquaintance deemed "suitable" by her family. "Most of my friends in Beijing had already married then because it was the thing to do," she says. Did she love him? Wu shrugs her shoulders and says, "I didn't find a better match at the time."

Although Wu and her parents had invested hundreds of thousands of renminbi in her RMB 1 million marital home, the property deed was in her husband's name alone, as is customary in China today. Wu, a litigator deeply familiar with the flaws in China's legal system, believed that a divorce lawsuit with an unyielding adversary would be lengthy and traumatic, with no guarantee of success. Rather than go through the court system, she decided to cut short her misery, let her husband keep all the assets, and pay him an additional RMB 100,000 in cash in exchange for his agreement to a divorce. At the time of their divorce in 2011, their marital home – which now belongs entirely to her ex-husband – had more than tripled in value to over RMB 3 million (around US$470,000 that year).

Wu refuses to marry again until she has bought a home in her own name, so that she can have more economic power and security within the relationship, which she believes would protect her from long-term abuse. "If I had had a home of my own when we were married, he never would have threatened me like that," she says.

Homes worth US$30 trillion, most registered in men's names

Like Wu, many Chinese women have been shut out of arguably the biggest accumulation of residential real-estate wealth in history, worth more than US$30 trillion in 2013. Even with tight regulations on buying property, China has the largest residential real-estate market in the world, with an urban home ownership rate of around 85 percent, according to China's central bank (though Gavekal Dragonomics says around three-fifths of urban residents own homes). Property is, by far, the biggest source of wealth in cities like Shanghai and Beijing. The only way that ordinary residents can afford to buy exorbitantly priced homes is by pooling assets.

That is, homes are financed by a combination of assets from husbands and wives, unmarried lovers, parents, aunts and uncles, grandparents, and other relatives or friends. But in a deeply patriarchal society, skyrocketing home prices mean that assets pooled from different family members tend to flow toward men.

A large body of evidence indicates that most residential property in China is owned by men. A 2012 Horizon Research and iFeng. com survey of thousands of home buyers in Beijing, Shanghai, Guangzhou, and Shenzhen found that men's names are on the property deeds of 80 percent of marital homes, but women's names are included on the deeds of only 30 percent of marital homes. My own research suggests that the gender asset gap is even larger when one considers how many homes are owned *solely* by men. At the time of writing, I had not found comprehensive data in China breaking down joint ownership versus sole ownership of homes; however, the nationwide Third Survey on the Social Status of Women in 2010 found that 51.7 percent of married men have sole ownership of the home, while only 13.2 percent of married women in China have homes in their own names. The 2010 quantitative survey, focusing specifically on gender differences in China, covered over 105,000 people aged 18 and over, and was carried out by the NBS and the All-China Women's Federation (comprehensive surveys on women were also carried out in 2000 and 1990).

Consider the enormous value of these primarily male-owned homes. A 2010 China research report by HSBC analysts Zhang Zhiming, Dilip Shahani, and Keith Chan estimated the total value of China's residential real-estate market to be more than RMB 109 trillion, or US$17 trillion. After 2010, NBS stopped publishing figures for the average home price in China. But HSBC analyst Zhang said in 2013 that the value of China's residential real-estate market is still around 3.3 times that of the country's gross domestic product (GDP). At the end of 2013, therefore, the value of homes in China exceeded RMB 187 trillion, or more than US$30 trillion.

The fact that most residential real-estate wealth is concentrated in the hands of men is the key reason why many Chinese feminist lawyers describe the Supreme People's Court's new interpretation of the Marriage Law in 2011 as a severe setback for women's property rights. The Marriage Law of 1950 was one of the first laws passed by the Communist government after the founding of the People's Republic of China, and it gave women many new rights, including the right to property. Although collectivization of land in subsequent years made property rights largely irrelevant in the 1960s and early 1970s, a 1980 amendment to the Marriage Law introduced special consideration for the rights and interests of the wife in disputed divorce settlements. Another amendment to the Marriage Law in 2001 made no mention of what should happen when only one party's name was registered on the property deed, emphasizing instead that "jointly possessed property is at the disposal of both spouses, on equal footing," according to Li Ying, an attorney and head of the Yuanzhong Gender Developent Center in Beijing, and women's rights attorney Guo Jianmei.

The 2011 interpretation of the Marriage Law by the Supreme People's Court, however, specifies that upon divorce, if both parties are unable to reach an agreement on the division of property, each side is entitled to keep whatever property is registered in his or her own name. Defenders argue that the new interpretation of the law is "gender-neutral." This may be so, but the consequences of the law are what scholars call "gender-specific." "This is a man's 'law'," writes attorney Li Ying. The Court's new interpretation "violates the Marriage Law's basic principle of common marital property," writes Li. That's because, as we have seen, most property deeds are in the man's name.

In theory, if a woman getting divorced can prove that she contributed financially to the down payment or mortgage payments on a home, she is entitled to compensation for the amount that she contributed, pro rata, over time. Yet very few women keep written records of how much money they have contributed to mortgage payments or to the down payment on the home. If any of these women end up divorcing, given the new interpretation of the Marriage Law, they would be hard-pressed to prove their right to a share of the home in a Chinese court.

It will likely take years of further analysis before we begin to understand the magnitude of this stunning reversal of women's property rights in China. The blow to women's property rights has profound consequences in other aspects of their lives, beyond losing out on the accumulation of wealth. Studies find that when battered women lack secure access to housing, they are more likely to remain trapped in an abusive relationship. Wu Mei – with her high income – was able to buy her way out of a violent marriage. Other abused women have no such option. The government has stalled on enacting targeted legislation to curb domestic violence, despite years of lobbying by feminist non-governmental organizations (NGOs). China in this regard lags behind other developing countries that have serious problems with violence against women, such as India and Bangladesh, which passed an anti-domestic-violence law in 2010. Official statistics state that one-quarter of China's women have experienced domestic violence (though activists say the real figure is much higher). Yet it is exceedingly difficult for a woman to gain protection from a violent partner. "Judges almost never define a case as 'domestic violence' because the current law in China is not specific or clear enough," says Feng Yuan, a leading activist with the Anti-Domestic Violence Network, an NGO in Beijing. "As a result, the courts routinely refer to domestic violence as 'family conflict' instead."

Wu Mei's story also illustrates the fact that even when the woman's income is extremely high, the man's bargaining power in the relationship is significantly enhanced by his sole ownership of the marital property, since the value of the home as an appreciating, fixed asset far exceeds one person's annual income. As a corporate attorney, Wu made much more money than her husband, yet she feels that it was the fact that their home was registered solely in her husband's name that gave him a sense of power over her, and made him feel free to abuse her because she had no other home to go to.

Wu's income did buy her a degree of power compared with other women, however. Wu says that several of her close female friends confided in her that they, too, were deeply unhappy in their marriages, and wished they could leave their husbands. "One night, we four friends were all eating dinner and crying at the same time," says Wu. "My friends think about divorcing, but my income is much higher, my living is guaranteed... they don't have the courage to divorce and lose everything like I did, they can't afford it so they don't do it." Yet many of these women may wind up divorced anyway. The divorce rate in large cities such as Beijing and Shanghai now exceeds 33 percent, while the nationwide divorce rate has risen for seven straight years, according to China's Ministry of Civil Affairs. The state media report that infidelity is the number one reason for divorce, while domestic violence ranks second.

Many men – and women as well – argue that a wife should have no claim to property purchased in the man's name prior to their marriage. Take Zhu Xin, a 25-year-old Shanghai resident and son of a property developer whom he described as "wealthy." I conduct most of my interviews one-on-one so that the woman or man can speak with complete anonymity about financial and emotional details of their relationship. But Zhu insisted on bringing along his wife, Yan Mei, also 25 years old, to dinner with me at a Taiwanese restaurant in 2012, just weeks after their wedding.

After we had chatted over appetizers, Zhu reached into his pocket and pulled out a document several pages long. It was a copy of the prenuptial contract he had written for his fiancée to sign. Zhu said he presented it to Yan three or four days before the wedding; then Yan interjected that she saw it for the first time just one day before they were scheduled to register their marriage legally. I looked at Yan's face for any signs of discomfort, but she had her arm cradled comfortably around his, as she listened patiently to Zhu's description of the negotiations preceding their marriage.

The prenuptial contract states that "all premarital property belongs solely to the party who purchased it." In addition, Zhu specifies that his wife will have no claim to property purchased *after* the marriage, either from his own savings or by his parents, unless she pays for the property with her own income. "Let's say we buy a home costing RMB 2 million; my parents pay 1 million, I pay 500,000, and my wife pays 500,000," said Zhu. "My parents would own 50 percent of the home, I would own 25 percent, and my wife would own 25 percent." Unlike Zhu, however, Yan has no assets, so it would be impossible for her to come up with the money to finance this hypothetical purchase.

Yan (woman): When he showed me the contract, I – and my parents, too – we were not particularly happy. It was like, our marriage is just a business. But then, I thought about the situation from his perspective. We discussed revising some of the clauses in the contract, and my parents made some suggestions…

Zhu (man): Because the contract lays out a kind of relationship between equals, there really are no unequal provisions in the agreement, so they were able to accept it.

Yan and her parents convinced Zhu to remove one clause declaring that he would keep 40 percent of his income for himself, and then Yan married him. Why did she feel such an urgent need to marry when she was just 25 years old and was unhappy with the prenuptial contract? Yan evaded the question, but her husband said: "her age is about the average marrying age for women, and she has pressure from her parents." The spectre of the "leftover" woman loomed again.

"He's going to be the landlord and I'll pay him rent"

The problem for women extends far beyond the fact that most homes are registered in the man's name alone. My research suggests that *many – if not most – of China's male-owned marital homes are heavily financed by the wife or girlfriend.* These are not just my own findings. Victor Yuan, chairman of Horizon Research, observed that the 2012 Horizon survey with iFeng.com of homebuyers in Beijing, Shanghai, Guangzhou and Shenzhen found that women contributed to the purchase of almost 90 percent of homes paid for in cash, and over 70 percent of homes bought with a mortgage loan.

As long as the woman is earning an income, she inevitably pays a significant portion of the monthly mortgage. Even if the woman does not transfer money from her own bank account to pay the mortgage directly, her income pays for other household expenses. In addition, many women contribute at least tens of thousands of renminbi – and often much more than RMB 100,000 – toward the down payment. Yet, even though they contribute heavily to the purchase of the home, many moderate- to high-income, university-educated women still allow the home to be registered solely in the man's name. Why are they so willing to give up their property rights? The underlying reasons are complicated, and have to do with the persistence of patriarchal norms, combined with the new dynamics of China's residential real-estate market.

Virtually every urban Chinese woman knows the saying *jiahan jiahan, chuanyi chifan* – "marry a man, marry a man, for clothes to wear, and food to eat." The widely perpetuated myth is that a woman must turn to a man for a home and all of life's essentials. This may have been true hundreds of years ago, but in today's China most women work very hard to make their own living. In fact, one of the legacies of the early Communist era is China's relatively high female labor-force participation rate; although this has now begun to fall significantly as a result of the dismantling of the planned economy and rising gender discrimination in hiring (see Chapter 1). Yet the state media continue to spread stereotypes concerning the avarice of women, which then become widely accepted as fact by men and women alike. Take the almost universally held notion that Chinese women refuse to marry a man unless he owns a home. Just as the media have inculcated in young women the belief that they must marry before they turn 27 or they will become "left over," they have bombarded men – and women – with the notion that Chinese women are overly greedy and materialistic.

In December 2010, a government Women's Federation-affiliated organization collaborated with the matchmaking website Baihe. com to conduct a nationwide survey of more than 30,000 people in thirty-one provinces on attitudes to marriage. In a write-up of the survey, the *People's Daily* website ran the headline "Survey Shows 70 percent of Chinese Women Say Man Must Own a House before Marriage." Since then, the notion that "70 percent of Chinese women seek to marry a man with a house" has been recycled through multiple state media reports and property sales advertisements. The *People's Daily* official survey write-up ran a cartoon showing a man kneeling before a woman, offering her a house in lieu of a bouquet of flowers.

My study finds no evidence, however, that the statistic published on the *People's Daily* website and in many other state media reports is accurate. I obtained the 2010 Marriage and Love Survey questionnaire: only one question was posed relating to men owning a home. This is how it appeared:

> Which economic traits should a man possess before he marries?
> (You may choose more than one)
>
> A Has a house ❑
>
> B Has a car ❑
>
> C Has a steady income ❑
>
> D Has some savings ❑
>
> E Parents have economic resources ❑
>
> F It doesn't matter ❑ [*wu suo wei*]

Given the way the question was constructed, it is possible that 70 percent of women taking this particular survey did indeed tick the A box (among others) and express a *desire* for their dream man to own a house before marriage.

Yet, in all my in-depth interviews and responses from hundreds of Weibo users, I have not found any examples of urban, educated women in their late twenties or older who *refused* to marry a man solely because he did not own a home. (One woman whose boyfriend treated her badly told me she used the fact that he did not own a house as an excuse to avoid marrying him.) On the contrary, I have found multiple examples of women in their twenties who are so worried about becoming "leftover" women that they rush into marriage without protecting their economic interests.

At the end of 2011, China's Ministry of Civil Affairs carried out another large-scale survey of over 50,000 people on love and marriage. The survey write-up on the Xinhua News website deployed the heading "'Leftover Women' Choosing Partners: No Money, No Deal – Having House is Top Priority." It again reported the frequently regurgitated statistic that, "in choosing a partner, 70 percent of women say that the man must have a house before marriage." It may be that some Chinese women try to demand that prospective suitors own a home as a condition of marriage, but I believe there are rather few educated women older than their late twenties whose sole reason for not marrying is that the man does not own a home.

It might be mere coincidence that most government surveys on "leftover" women and marriage are sponsored by matchmaking agencies. Or, more likely, the matchmaking industry is making a fortune from these state media reports about men needing to buy homes to find a bride and women needing to get married before they turn 27. Meanwhile, the notion that a man must own a home to placate the woman or future mother-in-law (*zhangmuniang*) plays a huge role in fueling consumer demand for residential real estate.

The 2012 Horizon and iFeng.com homebuyer survey on China's top real-estate markets also bears this out. Horizon chairman Victor Yuan says that many young men believe the media hype that the *zhangmuniang* will not let her daughter get married unless the boyfriend buys a home. "But we can see from the numbers that this is not what really happens," said Yuan at an iFeng.com media event in October 2012:

> As soon as the daughter turns 26, she enters a time of crisis. By the time the daughter turns 28, this feeling turns to fear and dread. So all you [men] have to do is put off the marriage until your girlfriend reaches age 27 or 28, then your *zhangmuniang* won't be worried anymore [about buying a house before marriage].

Yuan said that another sure-fire way for a young man who doesn't own a home to secure the parents' permission to marry their daughter is to get her pregnant: "The woman's parents will feel a sense of crisis that far outweighs concerns on the man's side, so it won't matter at all if you marry without owning a home."

Curiously, China's National Population and Family Planning Commission 2012–13 survey of over 98,000 people on love and marriage, sponsored by the matchmaking website Jiayuan.com, revised its figures downward to claim that 52 percent of women say a man must own a house before marriage – perhaps a sign that even the state media cannot get away with disseminating blatant untruths year after year.

Unfortunately, because of the lack of reliable statistics from the Chinese government, many reputable foreign news organizations and even scholars take these biased surveys about women and report them as fact. One anecdote has made the rounds of virtually every news organization in the world: a woman appearing on the television dating show *If You Are the One* famously said in 2010,

"I'd rather cry in the back of a BMW than smile on the back of a bicycle." This one remark is regularly pulled out by journalists as proof of the outrageous greed of Chinese women. What the journalists fail to mention is that these television shows are heavily *scripted*. One of the guests who appeared on *If You Are the One* told me that the show producer fed them lines, which they were required to memorize and recite on the air as a condition of being selected.

Some young women talk at length about how greedy other Chinese women are in general, but see themselves as the exception to the rule. Take 26-year-old Lu Ling, a graduate with a B.A. in sociology from a reputable university in Beijing, who was shopping for a home with her fiancé when I interviewed her in 2012. Lu believed that the 2011 Supreme People's Court's new interpretation of the Marriage Law was good for society. Why? "Chinese women need to learn to be more independent, and stop relying on men to meet all their needs," she said, parroting a line that appears often in the media. Yet Lu herself planned to leave her name off the marital property deed. She said she was contributing her savings of tens of thousands of renminbi toward the down payment on the home, and also planned to pay half of the mortgage payment each month. Lu wouldn't even discuss the subject of adding her name to the property deed with her boyfriend, however, because his family would be contributing much more money toward the down payment. I asked Lu if she thought it was unfair for the home to be registered solely in the man's name, even though she was financing it as well. "Of course it's fair," Lu said, laughing brightly at my suggestion that there might be anything wrong with the arrangement. "He's going to be the landlord and I'll pay him rent." Lu's future husband will also be the only one to benefit from any appreciation in the value of the marital home.

Not all women are so blithe about signing away their legal property rights. My research suggests that one of the key reasons why so many women marrying after 2006 are willing to give up ownership of the marital home is that they are afraid of becoming "leftover" and jeopardizing their chances of ever finding another husband if they assert their will. These women recognize that they are likely to lose out in the future if their name is not included on the property deed, so they may speak up for themselves at first, but later back down under pressure from their husband or boyfriend and other family members – including in some cases their own parents, who are extremely anxious to see their daughters marry.

Take Wang Li, a 25-year-old Communist Party member and university graduate, with a coveted job and generous benefits at China's Public Security Bureau in Beijing. In 2011, she took her life savings of RMB 60,000 (almost US$10,000 that year) and gave it to her boyfriend to help buy an apartment in his name alone in preparation for marriage. The couple originally wanted to rent a place, but the parents on both sides said they must first purchase a marital home. Wang is an only child, but her parents did not give her money because they expected the man's family to provide the home. The boyfriend's parents had saved RMB 200,000 for the deposit, and they insisted that the home be registered solely in the man's name.

"I won't hide it from you," Wang says. "My boyfriend and I started to quarrel." They argued for months over the home registration and Wang was so angry that she almost called off the wedding. Wang's own mother urged her to stop fighting with her boyfriend and to just let him have formal ownership of the home. But Wang continued to waver. Then, her boyfriend's mother called her in tears, saying that Wang's professional success (her total compensation package from work exceeded that of her boyfriend) threatened the security of the upcoming marriage. Her boyfriend's mother said that in order to give him a sense of security (*baozhang*), it was very important to register the home in the man's name. "His mother started crying on the phone and I thought, forget it, whatever works is fine," Wang says. She then agreed to register the home in her boyfriend's name and they got married.

Wang had been tempted to walk away from the wedding because of the unequal financial arrangement. She was only 25 years old and still had time to find another, more egalitarian relationship, so why did she give up? Throughout our 2½-hour-long interview, Wang exuded self-confidence and displayed no sign of regret that she had given up on her fight to register the marital home in her name alongside that of her now husband:

> I really think it doesn't matter now. If someday we don't have feelings for each other, the marital property won't matter to me. I have the ability to find another house on my own. Some young women complain [if their name is not on the property deed] because their own guarantee is gone and they feel insecure. But this money is not important to me. If all of this goes to him only, it's OK.

Actually, it's not OK. It may be impossible to tease out the final, psychological barrier Wang had to overcome to give up her demand for equal rights to the marital property. But even if her marriage does not end in divorce, the fact that her husband now has complete control over the valuable marital property significantly enhances his power in the relationship. A large body of research derived from exchange theory and game theory demonstrates that if one partner (and that is generally the woman) is economically dependent on another, the dependent one has less power in the marriage.

Sociologist Mariko Lin Chang explains in her book *Shortchanged: Why Women Have Less Wealth and What Can Be Done About It:*

> [W]hen husbands earn more than wives, the wives are financially dependent and less able to support themselves if the marriage ends. As a consequence of their greater financial dependency, women will be less likely to leave a marriage than men will, a hesitancy that renders them less powerful within the marriage and more likely to capitulate when conflict arises. In exchange for the economic benefits of marriage, women are more likely to do the least desirable household tasks (such as cleaning toilets, changing diapers etc.), defer financial decisions to their husbands, and put their own career choices second to their husband's.

Moreover, in China, property prices at the time of writing continue to rise, so a woman who gives up ownership of the home is losing out on the investment potential of the marital property; property restrictions and mortgage loan laws are constantly changing, meaning that she may not be able to obtain a new loan on her own, regardless of her income; and she may end up losing her job, which would make her even more vulnerable.

In Wang Li's case, her professional success was greater than her husband's, so her husband's masculinity was injured because he was not the household's primary breadwinner. Complicating matters even further, in China today home ownership is a defining feature of masculinity. Anthropologist Li Zhang observes in her book *In Search of Paradise: Middle-Class Living in a Chinese Metropolis* that men are expected to be head of the household and the official homeowner, such that the practice of *daochamen*, where the man moves into his wife's home, is considered "somewhat disgraceful." Wang Li felt that in order to compensate for her success in the workplace, she had to cede ownership of her most valuable asset – her home – to her husband alone.

Many studies – including Arlie Russell Hochschild's *The Second Shift* and Veronica Jaris Tichenor's *Earning More and Getting Less: Why Successful Wives Can't Buy Equality* – have demonstrated that women's incomes have not necessarily bought them greater power within their marriages. Wives with higher earnings disrupt a traditionally gendered balance of power within the marriage, so in Euro-American countries some wives compensate by taking on more household work. In China, successful professional women may not compensate by doing more housework because of the availability of cheap domestic help; but some of them do so by letting their less successful husband claim sole ownership of the home.

In cases where the woman has not contributed directly to the deposit on a home, the woman's family is often expected to pay for all of the renovations (*zhuangxiu*) of the "naked" apartment to make it suitable for living. The cost of these renovations often equals or even exceeds the cost of the down payment. Buying a home in China is not like in the USA or Europe, where generally the home could be expected to have floors, toilets, sinks, plaster on the walls and electrical outlets. In China, one buys a bare concrete space, so it requires a tremendous investment to turn this cavity, which lacks the most basic amenities, into an actual home.

Yet, in the gendered hierarchy of home buying in China, the man's family contribution to the deposit is seen to "count" toward the actual home purchase, while the woman's family contribution to the fitting out of the concrete space does not "count", even though the dollar amount may be the same given that the work includes everything from electrical wiring, plumbing, heating/air conditioning, flooring and furnishings and fixtures. Money is fungible, after all. In addition to paying for expensive fitting out (essential before the house can be actually lived in), a woman's income may go toward a car, or other living expenses such as groceries, doctor's visits, transportation and education, while the man's money goes toward building equity in an appreciating fixed asset. But far too many women and men say it would not be "fair" for the woman to include her name on the marital home deed next to the man's name because they believe that the woman's contribution does not count as much as the man's.

For example, when Shanghai resident Hong Lei and her boyfriend began discussing marriage in 2005, her boyfriend's parents made a down payment of RMB 186,000 on a RMB 930,000 (US$113,000 in 2005) home, registered in their son's name. Hong's boyfriend set up an automatic debit from his bank account so his monthly salary would go straight toward paying the mortgage, while the two of them lived on Hong's salary. They married less than a year after the home purchase. When the concrete contours of the "naked apartment" (*maopifang*) were built, Hong used her RMB 120,000 (US$14,000) in savings to pay for fittings, furniture and appliances to make the new home habitable. She also began contributing to the monthly mortgage payments as soon as they married, since, although her husband's income was higher than hers, he still needed or wanted her to contribute. Meanwhile, Hong's own parents declined to give her money to help buy a home because they considered it the man's responsibility to provide it, so they instead gave money to her male cousin to help him buy a home:

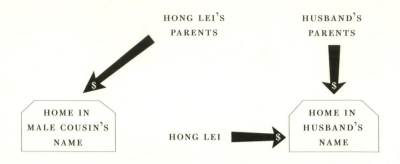

Hong, a 32-year-old fund manager, with a 4-year-old daughter when I interviewed her in 2012, estimates that the home has appreciated by over 300 percent to more than RMB 3 million (around US$480,000 in 2012). (Needless to say, it is worth even more now.) Yet she still does not wish to ask her husband to add her name to the deed. "I don't care too much about real estate," she said. "Besides, his parents paid the deposit on the home and it would not be fair to add my name," she added, echoing other women I have interviewed.

Hong does not consider that her parents-in-law only contributed RMB 66,000 (US$8,000 in 2005) more than she did toward the home at the very beginning. She discounts all those years in which she paid half of the mortgage payments, while her husband's parents did not pay anything. Nor does she consider the fact that her husband did not pay anything toward the deposit because his parents paid for his portion, while her contribution toward the down payment came entirely from her own savings. She simply accepts the prevailing patriarchal notion that the man should be the official homeowner.

"I have been cast aside by the law"

While some women believe "it would not be fair" to add their name to the marital home deed, many others express a strong desire to do so, but face overwhelming pressure to give up their attempt to achieve gender equity.

Consider Meng Jian, a 30-year-old Shanghai resident, Communist Party member, only daughter, and Ph.D. candidate in sociology at a top university. Meng is the very embodiment of some of the ways in which women have become empowered in post-socialist China: she is striving for the very best through her choice to pursue a Ph.D., her membership of the elite Communist Party, and her career ambitions. But as soon as Meng began thinking about marrying and buying a home, she fell victim to new and powerful forces perpetuating gender inequality.

Meng's boyfriend was a financial analyst. In 2009 he urged her to buy a home in Shanghai with him because real-estate prices were climbing so fast. "I didn't want to buy at first because I'm only a student, but he said we had to buy before we got married, otherwise home prices would be too expensive for us," said Meng. (It is worth noting that buying a home early made good economic sense for the man on account of the hot real-estate market.) Her boyfriend was busy working long hours at the office, so Meng went by herself to look at apartments in downtown Shanghai, near her boyfriend's office, settled on one that she liked, and called him to see it. He liked it as well, so their real-estate agent negotiated with the landlord and settled on a final price of RMB 2.8 million (around US$410,000 in 2009). Meng and her parents contributed RMB 400,000 (around US$59,000 in 2009) toward the deposit, and her boyfriend and his parents contributed an equal amount.

In this regard, Meng's parents were more progressive than some other parents of daughters in urban China, who decline to contribute any money at all toward their daughter's home purchase. Then came time to register names on the property deed.

"I wanted my name on the home deed, but it was very inconvenient [*mafan*] to do all the paperwork since we weren't married, so it was easier for us just to put his name down," said Meng. If the bureaucratic procedure for buying a home were not so complicated, requiring the involvement of people and institutions in addition to Meng and her boyfriend, Meng would have added her name to the deed. But the real-estate agent told Meng and her boyfriend that, since they were not yet married, it would be easier for them just to put the man's name on the deed, and Meng relented because of the perceived urgency of buying a home before prices rose any higher (they could, after all, have married before finalizing the home sale). Her boyfriend suggested they call Meng's mother to see if it was acceptable to put his name alone on the deed. Her mother said yes, because they could always add Meng's name to the deed later. When Meng's mother entered the sales transaction, her retrograde beliefs about gender – that it did not matter if her daughter's name was on the property deed – further inhibited Meng's own desire to include her name on the deed.

Meng married her boyfriend in July 2011. One month later, China's Supreme Court amended the Marriage Law, and Meng knew immediately that this meant her marital home belonged solely to her new husband in the eyes of the law. "I panicked and felt very frightened, so I talked to him about adding my name to the property deed," said Meng. But her husband said they should wait until they bought a second home, and register her name solely on that deed instead. That way, he argued, they could avoid paying the higher down payment required when buying a second home, part of new regulatory controls imposed in 2010 on property purchases. Her husband's argument made sense to Meng, so she has given up asking him to add her name to the deed.

"I do have lingering worries about our home, but my husband is a good person and I can trust him," said Meng. The final barrier to Meng's realization of her desire for gender equality in home ownership proved to be the state regulations on home buying, which are supposedly gender-neutral, but in fact have gender-specific consequences. The 2010 government regulation imposing a higher down payment requirement for the purchase of second homes – while intended to control property prices – had the consequence of imposing new obstacles to women's property rights: what woman would insist on adding her name to the property deed alongside that of her husband if it means that the couple will have to pay much more money for their next home? The only way to avoid the second-home penalty is to put the home *in the woman's name only* (and couples rarely do this).

When I asked Meng if they were planning to buy a second home, however, Meng said that they cannot afford to buy because it is too expensive. If Meng felt very strongly about writing her name on the property deed, she could argue with her husband that it was worth it to jump over the bureaucratic hurdles involved, since they cannot afford to buy a second home anyway. Instead, the social and regulatory forces working against her effectively crushed her desire for gender equality. Even if Meng manages to buy a second home in the future, with her name solely on the deed, she will still have missed out on the tremendous appreciation in the value of the first marital home bought in 2009, which is registered solely in her husband's name. Most analysts at the time of writing argue that the greatest wealth-building period of China's real estate boom is already over.

Meanwhile, since Meng's two-bedroom home is registered solely in her husband's name, her in-laws live with her most of the year and treat the home as their own, keeping close tabs on Meng's movements. "I don't have any freedom. Today, when I came to meet you for our interview, I had to leave a note for my in-laws telling them where I was going and when I would return," said Meng. Meng says that her own parents – who contributed just as much money to the home as her in-laws did – do not feel entitled to stay in the home for more than a week or so, once or twice a year.

Zhang Fan, a 29-year-old Beijing resident, only daughter and Ph.D. candidate, paid RMB 350,000 (US$55,000) of the down payment on a home registered solely in her boyfriend's name before they married in 2010. Zhang, who is also a Communist Party member, says she wanted to put her name on the deed, but the real-estate agent said that only one person's name was allowed, and she believed him. (I have heard from other buyers that real-estate agents sometimes warn the man to "think very carefully about the consequences" before he allows the woman to register her name jointly on the deed, but I do not have adequate supportive data on this point.) She, too, did not think any more about the property registration until China's Supreme Court issued its 2011 interpretation of the Marriage Law, which meant that Zhang would have difficulty proving her claim to the property, despite her hefty financial contribution to its purchase.

"I feel that I have been cast aside by the law," said Zhang. "I thought long and hard about how to bring up the subject of adding my name to the deed with my husband, and I was really torn [*jiujie*]," she said. When I interviewed Zhang in January 2012, she was very worried about losing the property if her marriage did not work out. But when I checked in with her again in late 2012, Zhang said that it wasn't worth disrupting her marital relationship by pressing the issue with her husband, so she still had not added her name to the deed.

These gendered dynamics in home ownership exist not only in the most expensive, "first-tier" cities of Beijing and Shanghai, but also in many other, so-called second- and third-tier, cities, where real estate is more affordable. For example, in the second-tier coastal city Dalian, Chen Liang paid RMB 60,000 toward the down payment on a home registered in her boyfriend's name before they married in 2009. Chen wrote to my Weibo account that in addition to contributing to the down payment, she also paid more than RMB 100,000 for fittings and that she shares mortgage payments with her husband. The home cost RMB 700,000 (US$103,000 that year) in 2009 but has now appreciated significantly in value. Chen, 30 years old, writes that she did not put her name on the deed because "the notion that 'the man is head of the family' is still with us." Chen now wishes she had registered her name. "I feel uncomfortable in my heart," she writes. But she has not raised the issue with her husband because "it is important to manage the marriage properly so it will last through our old age."

Young women in their twenties getting married for the first time are often caught up in the excitement of the wedding and can hardly be faulted for failing to predict the long-term consequences of giving away their property rights. Yet their lives often become much more difficult after marrying and having a child. Consider that in 2010 the average working woman in China spent 2½ to 3 times longer on household chores than men, according to official statistics. Yet studies show that most married men and women in China do not challenge the gendered division of housework. The gender divisions become even starker if the wife gives up her job to raise a child, and the consequences of the Court's new interpretation of the Marriage Law are especially dire for women who are stay-at-home mothers, not earning any income. These women are not seen to be contributing financially to the household in any way.

The dependent situation of wives and mothers who are not working is exacerbated by the fact that most Chinese state banks do not allow joint accounts. Therefore most women, who by and large make less money than men, do not know how their husbands manage their bank accounts and other assets. Mariko Lin Chang writes in *Shortchanged*:

> If one partner retains complete control over assets, it is possible for him or her to hide assets or mask a bad financial situation. The dissipation of marital assets (for example, wasting assets or transferring them to a third party) can influence divorce settlements, but in order to demonstrate that marital assets were dissipated, one must have knowledge about the types and the extent of marital assets over the duration of the marriage.

Even if, as in some cases, a husband lets his wife use his bank debit card to go shopping, the woman has no control over the assets. She is unable to perform many teller transactions at the bank because the account is not her own, and she would be left completely vulnerable if something happened to her husband, or if he decided to leave her.

Take Zhang Yuan, a former advertising agency art director in Beijing. After graduating from university, she advanced rapidly in her field and gladly logged long hours at the office. Zhang took out a mortgage on a Beijing home with her husband in 2005 for a total value of RMB 250,000 (US$30,000 in 2005) – a bargain by today's standards. Even though she contributed to the down payment and shared mortgage payments with her husband, she agreed to register the home under his name alone because she "trusted him." Meanwhile, she was so dedicated to her career that she didn't have a child until she had turned 33 – considered quite late in China. "I loved my work, but I didn't like the way my parents spoiled my son, so I decided to take care of him myself," says Zhang.

But at age 37, Zhang has been unable to find a job remotely equivalent to the one she used to have, and after two years of sending out résumés and attending interviews, she has become increasingly pessimistic about ever restarting her career. She has not given up on her job search, but housework, shopping and cooking take up most of her days now while her son is at school. Since she has no income of her own and does not share a bank account with her husband, Zhang uses her husband's debit card when she goes shopping. This gives her a feeling of security (*anquan gan*). Still, when China's Supreme Court issued its new interpretation of the Marriage Law in 2011, Zhang became anxious about the fact that her name was not on the marital property deed. "This law is so unfair to women, and so unfair to mothers. We're the ones who have to raise the child," she says.

Zhang approached her husband about adding her name to the property deed, but he told her it was too inconvenient (*mafan*) given all the paperwork required and she dropped the subject. When I asked her whether she would raise the issue of property registration with her husband in the future, she insisted that "it doesn't really matter anymore." Meanwhile, the home registered solely in her husband's name had appreciated by a whopping 800 percent since they bought it, and was worth around RMB 2 million in 2012 (around US$317,000 at that time). Zhang would be in a particularly vulnerable position if her marriage ends in divorce, as more and more marriages in China now do. As with many other women who missed out on the initial wealth-building period of the real-estate boom, even if Zhang were to get a highpaying job now and manage to buy a home in her own name, she will never be able to get back into the real-estate investment game in an equivalent way.

Not all homes are registered solely in the man's name. Roughly a quarter of married women and men jointly own a home with their spouse, according to the 2010 Third Survey on the Social Status of Women carried out by the All-China Women's Federation and the NBS. Yet even when a married couple have an egalitarian relationship, with the names of both husband and wife registered jointly on the property deed (meaning that, unless otherwise specified, the property is technically owned 50:50), China's bank regulations may still work against the woman.

Take the relationship of Du Xin and Ye Fan, both lawyers in Shanghai, who married in 2008 and bought a home in 2009 for RMB 1.5 million (around US$220,000 then), with a down payment of RMB 700,000 (around US$103,000). Du, the 37-year-old husband, paid RMB 250,000; Ye, his 35-year-old wife, paid the same; and Ye asked her parents to pay the difference of RMB 200,000, because her husband's parents were farmers with very little money. I spoke with Du and Ye for almost two hours at a Shanghai café in 2013. They were very excited about having just paid off the entire mortgage on their home, and the husband brought along a thick bundle of financial documents, detailing the payments they had made on their home over the years. When I asked why they decided to register both their names on the deed when so many couples put down just the man's name, here is how they responded:

Ye (woman): It was very natural to put both of our names on the deed.

Du (man): Yes, two names are on the deed, but the first name is mine, as the household head.

Ye: Really? (laughs)

Du: The first name is mine.

Ye: Actually…

Du: [interrupting] Yes, the property deed says my name first… I am the primary loan recipient… she is the secondary loan recipient.

Since Du is the "primary loan recipient" in this case, the mortgage loan company views the man as the person who has a greater stake in the property. Moreover, the man's bank account was set up to make automatic mortgage payments, while the couple used the woman's account primarily for other living expenses such as food, transport and entertainment. In addition, the couple made one-time transactions of RMB 200,000 (around US$32,000 at the 2012 exchange rate) a few times a year to pay down the principal on the mortgage. Ye said it was extremely complicated for them both to transfer money to pay down the mortgage, so each time they made a big one-time payment she withdrew cash from her bank account and deposited it in her husband's account. Then Du would wire the money to the mortgage lender. As a result, all of the receipts documenting mortgage payments recorded only the man's name.

According to the new interpretation of the Marriage Law, if this couple were to divorce, the legal documentation about house payments would only show the man's financial contribution, not that of the woman. In the event of a legal dispute over the property division, this would put a heavier burden of proof on the woman to show that she participated equally in paying the mortgage on the home, even though her name was listed on the property deed. (See Chapter 5 for details of a divorce case where the court awarded an abused wife only 30 percent of the home value in the settlement, even though her name was jointly on the property deed.)

When I asked the couple if they had thought of setting up a joint bank account to make payments easier, Ye asked, "What is a joint bank account?" Out of my entire study of 283 people, I have not encountered a single person who had a joint urban bank account with their spouse or significant other. As of September 2013, major banks such as China Merchants Bank and Bank of China do not permit couples to open a joint bank account. This separation of the finances of married couples is another way in which the Chinese regulatory system effectively reinforces the patriarchal norm of the man as household head, again showing that a gender-neutral regulation can have gender-specific consequences.

I interviewed another woman in Shanghai who had joint ownership of the marital home with her husband. But the husband turned out to be extremely violent, and in the end she was forced to give up her home, in spite of having her name jointly on the property deed (see Chapter 5 on intimate partner violence). In China's current legal environment, it appears that only women with *sole* ownership of a home have true control over the property.

This chapter has shown how even though much of China's US$30 trillion in residential real estate has been heavily financed through the hard-earned savings of women, most of the property is owned by men. My research has found that many Chinese women have transferred their assets to their boyfriend or husband to buy a marital home – and are often encouraged to do so by their parents – even though the home tends to be registered solely in the man's name. Although some women simply do not question the custom of the man as household head and homeowner, many others have a strong desire to register their names on the marital home deed, but they back down in the face of overwhelming social and regulatory obstacles.

Many women marrying in 2007 or later (when the "leftover" women media campaign began) have given up their property rights when they married specifically because they were afraid of becoming "leftover" women, too "old" to find another husband. The Chinese state media effort to stigmatize single, educated women in their late twenties as "leftover" women is therefore not just a curious cultural phenomenon. The insights of feminist critic and philosopher Judith Butler in her 1998 *New Left Review* essay, "Merely Cultural," are particularly relevant to understanding the effects of the "leftover" women campaign: "It would be a mistake to understand such productions as 'merely cultural' if they are essential to the functioning of the sexual order of political economy, that is, if they constitute a fundamental threat to its very workability."

The extraordinary pressure on educated women to marry has had damaging economic consequences because so many women have been afraid to walk away from an unequal financial arrangement with their boyfriend or husband. Women not yet married were unwilling to break off the engagement if their fiancé did not add their name to the deed. And married women often feared that insisting that their husband add their name to the deed might jeopardize the relationship.

While this chapter has focused on gender inequality within marriage, Chapter 3 broadens out beyond marriage to examine gender inequality within the extended family and the reasons behind middle-class Chinese consumers' obsession with buying real estate. It explains how many Chinese parents discriminate against their own daughters and tend to buy homes for sons only. China's privatization of housing and subsequent real-estate mania over the past decade and a half has had profound consequences for all Chinese women and men – including LGBTQ communities and others in non-traditional relationships in China – and has contributed to the creation of unprecedented gender inequality in wealth.

THREE

China's giant gender wealth gap

China's privatization of housing and skyrocketing home prices over the past decade have created new forms of inequity, based on class and on *hukou* or household registration, which restricts the privileges residents receive (such as education or health care) according to their birthplace (see Box). But I argue that the greatest inequality of all generated by the country's real-estate boom is along gender lines. Post-socialist China's privatization of housing since 1998 has resulted in an unprecedented and fast accumulation of residential real-estate wealth, yet this wealth is out of reach for those women whose families are unwilling to help them make the down payment on an urban home.

Consider the case of Guo Yuan, a sales manager in Shanghai, who felt in control of her destiny until she turned 28. An only child, Guo had saved tens of thousands of renminbi in the years after she graduated from university and hoped to realize her dream of home ownership by making a down payment on an apartment in her own name. Then her parents persuaded her to help her male cousin in Jiangxi province buy a house instead. "My *biaoge* is already 34 and has been unable to find a wife," said Guo, referring to her older male cousin. "My parents thought that if we helped him buy a home, he might be able to get married."

The *hukou* system

China's *hukou* system, tying an individual firmly to place of household registration, dates back to around 1960, when "'invisible walls' Mao and his colleagues had created around Chinese cities slammed shut their doors," according to sociologist Martin King Whyte in *One Country, Two Societies*:

> At birth an individual inherited the household registration
> status of his or her mother (although China is a thoroughly
> patrilineal society by tradition) and was classified as agricultural
> or nonagricultural, as well as by the level of city for anyone with
> nonagricultural *hukou*. Registration status was tied to a complex
> set of migration restrictions… Permission to migrate upward
> in the system was granted only if the urban destination gave
> bureaucratic approval in advance, and that was granted only in
> relatively rare and special situations (for example, admission to an
> urban university, service in and then demobilization from the army
> as an officer, or in a situation in which an urban factory had taken
> over rural land for plant expansion).

One of the major consequences of China's reforms in the post-Mao era is the loosening of migration restrictions. As part of China's privatization of housing in 1998, some cities such as Shanghai introduced incentives for people to buy homes, so they offered anyone purchasing a home an opportunity to obtain a *hukou* in the city. When home prices began rising rapidly, Shanghai canceled its program giving new home buyers a city *hukou*, but most cities still allowed anyone to purchase a home, free of restrictions. Then in 2010, China's State Council introduced nationwide guidelines to local governments on how to restrict the purchase of homes in an attempt to prevent the residential property market from overheating. It became much more difficult for residents of many cities to buy a home, but particularly in Beijing, which now has the most draconian home-buying requirements in the country. Following the 2010 government restrictions on property purchases, household registration or *hukou* is again assuming a greater role in rural–urban inequality.

Guo's parents declined to help her make the down payment on a home because they thought that, as a woman, she did not need to own property. Her male cousin in Jiangxi, however, was expected to be a homeowner. Guo herself felt no loyalty or affection for her cousin, but she felt a deep sense of filial piety toward her parents. When she gave her cousin the money for his house, she was demonstrating her loyalty to her parents, as is customary according to Chinese tradition. Guo had only one request: "Let's get a simple home for him, not too expensive, because we don't have too much money," she told her mother.

On top of abandoning her dream of buying a home in favor of helping a cousin she did not particularly like, Guo decided that she had to marry quickly, because at age 28 she had crossed the threshold for becoming a "leftover" woman. She accepted a proposal from a man she had met three months earlier. Even though she loves her job managing sales for an IT company, she turned down a lucrative promotion offer, which would have required more travel. "It is most difficult for men to accept [a woman] doing this kind of job," said Guo. Asked why she felt the need to marry so quickly, she said:

> The best time for a woman to marry really is around age 25. You can wait a little longer to have a child, but this is the unavoidable truth. A couple of years ago, I couldn't figure it out. Especially when I watched those Western movies, I felt very free and easy. I thought, why is everyone so worried about my being single? But in these last two years my attitude has changed. We are members of society, after all. It's really hard to prevent everyone around you from affecting you, unless you are very, very strong in your heart and you just don't care at all what anyone else thinks.

Guo's story illustrates yet another way in which women are shut out of home ownership and wealth accumulation in

China: Chinese parents routinely discriminate against their own daughters when it comes to helping family members buy a home.

Why parents tend to buy homes for sons but not daughters

My research reveals that while parents are willing to make great financial sacrifices to help their son buy a home, parents of daughters often decline to help buy a home, even if they have the means to do so. (By "help buy a home" I mean either giving cash or providing a no-interest loan with no time limit for repayment, either for the entire cost of the apartment or for the legally required deposit.) In hundreds of interviews I conducted online and in person, I didn't come across a single case where parents with a son and daughter helped their daughter buy a home with no conditions but did not help their son, if he planned to marry. I canvassed my acquaintances and posted on my Weibo account a request for such examples, but to no avail. By contrast, I found at least twenty cases where parents helped buy a home for their son but declined to help their marriage-age daughter.

For example, Shao Li is a 32-year-old real-estate sales manager in Beijing with two brothers in Hohhot, Inner Mongolia. Her parents bought homes for both of her brothers before they married, but would not contribute to the down payment on her home when she married, simply because she is female. In retelling the story, Shao said that her mother was the one who took care of the financial arrangements for her brothers. After her mother finished buying them homes, she said: "Now that my sons are married with their own homes, I have fulfilled all my obligations."

I asked Shao if she thought she had been treated unfairly, but she repeatedly said no:

LHF: Did you ever say to your mother, "You might also help me buy a home"?

Shao: No, I never said that.

LHF: Did you ever feel…

Shao [interrupting]: No, I never felt that.

LHF: Did you ever feel that it was unfair?

Shao: I feel it was very fair. Because I'm a daughter, after all. If I had been a son, of course my mother would have found a way to buy a home for me too. Because I'm a daughter, she didn't. I feel this is fair. This is just deep-rooted Chinese tradition; this is just the way it is.

When so many women are raised to believe that it is only fair for their parents to help their brother or male cousin buy a home because they are male, the same women are likely to believe that it is only fair for the boyfriend or husband to have sole ownership of a home, even though the women may have heavily financed the home purchase. Like many other women in China, Shao used all her savings to help pay the deposit on a home registered solely in her boyfriend's name in 2008.

Shao: My boyfriend's family doesn't have much money, so he borrowed money from friends, I borrowed money from friends, and I also used my own savings to make the down payment. He said we could put my name on the deed, but I thought that I should be fair, because this money didn't all come from me, and I haven't married him yet. If we were to split up in the future, and I were to say "this house is mine and you can't have it," well, I couldn't really justify that.

LHF: So this house belongs entirely to your boyfriend? Shao: Yes.

LHF: And you think this is fair?

Shao: Yes.

I found at least nine cases where parents paid in full (leaving no mortgage debt) for urban homes for their son, but I did not find a single case out of 283 people where parents paid in full for a home for their daughter. One Beijing resident in his early fifties explained why he paid in full for an apartment for his 11-year-old son: "I don't want him to become a poor sod (*qiong xiaozi*), who can't get a girlfriend." A 55-year-old Shanghai chauffeur, Zhan Yang, similarly paid in full for a small apartment in Shanghai for his only son in 2008, when the son was not yet married and only 22 years old. Zhan complained about how much money he had had to spend on his son because men were expected to own a home. "If I had a daughter instead of a son, I wouldn't have had to spend nearly as much money on her," he said.

Or take Zhou Nan, a 25-year-old man who works as a hair stylist in Beijing. He has two older sisters. His parents did not help his sisters buy homes, even when they married. Yet even though Zhou had no plans to marry, his parents bought him a new apartment outright, in cash, several years ago. Then they helped him pay the deposit on a *second* apartment in his own name. Asked why his parents did not help his sisters, Zhou said: "Chinese parents do not like to buy homes for girls."

My findings help explain the larger, nationwide pattern in a survey of over 105,000 people conducted by the All-China Women's Federation and NBS in 2010, showing that only one in every fifteen single women owned their own home (6.9 percent), compared with one in five single men (21.8 percent).

Blatant parental favoring of sons over daughters in buying valuable, residential real estate is important because the Chinese government is phasing out its draconian one-child policy (enforced since 1980). In the future, more and more sisters are likely to have to compete with their brothers for parental investment. The Chinese government announced in March 2013 that the agency formerly in charge of the one-child policy, the National Population and Family Planning Commission, would merge with the Ministry of Health. Then, in November, the Communist Party followed up with an official statement that China will now allow couples to have two children if either the husband or wife is an only child. Demographer Wang Feng, who has extensively researched China's one-child policy, wrote that "the world's most controversial birth-control policy, initially imposed as an emergency measure at the start of the economic reforms of Deng Xiaoping, seems to finally be on its way out…"

Moreover, even before the whittling away of the one-child policy, roughly two-thirds of Chinese couples were not bound by one-child-policy restrictions, according to demographers Wang, Cai Yong and Gu Baochang. Urban middle-class couples have long been able to circumvent restrictions in various ways, such as paying a fine. Millions of rural residents have also been exempted from the one-child restrictions and rural couples were often allowed to have more than one child if their first baby was a girl. China's rapid urbanization has resulted in millions of women and men with rural or smaller town household registration (*hukou*) who have moved to a large city and have siblings. The decades-old *hukou* system placed strict limits on the ability of China's population to move from the countryside to the city, but following the government's privatization of housing in 1998 many rural residents were allowed to obtain an urban *hukou* if they bought a home in the city. As long as they could afford it, these were the people who bought urban homes over the past decade and a half, along with people born in the city, who were more likely to be from only-child families.

While the erosion of the one-child policy is welcome news, it may lead to even more conspicuous parental favoring of sons over daughters in home buying, unless current trends change. Not only do parents favor their son over their daughter in home buying, they often pressure their daughter into helping them buy the brother (or male cousin) a home. Anthropologist Wang Danning writes that there has been an increase in urban women supporting their brothers financially, since the brother is viewed as "the child of the family as a whole, for whom all members of the extended family share responsibility."

Most young men and women in China continue to feel a deep sense of filial piety and obligation to the family. Even if a man is initially in favor of adding his wife's name to the deed of the marital home, his loyalty still tends to lie with his parents and other relatives who have contributed more money toward the deposit, so the man often ends up siding with his parents rather than the woman he is marrying. A woman's sense of obligation to her family may compel her to pass up the opportunity of buying a home of her own in favor of helping her male relative financially. And even if she feels no loyalty to the male relative, her sense of filial piety may compel her to give money to her parents, who then give it to the male relative.

Just as some only daughters consider it their family duty to help their male cousins financially, women with brothers frequently consider it their duty to help them, and indeed some would rather help their brother buy a home than buy one for themselves. Take 37-year-old Zhang Jing in Nanchang, a city in the southeastern province of Jiangxi, who has a brother six years younger. Zhang wrote me long private communications, sent to my Weibo account, telling me that when she married neither her parents nor her brother helped her buy her home. Yet in 2005, she paid most of the RMB 180,000 (US$22,000 in 2005) deposit on her brother's home. Her parents helped him as well. In 2008, she transferred another RMB 60,000 (US$8,800 then) to help pay off the rest of her brother's mortgage so that he could marry his girlfriend. "If the woman heard that my brother did not own a home, she probably would not want him," she said. Zhang's brother later married – and his home is registered solely in his name.

I conducted in-depth interviews with sixteen women who said that their parents did not contribute money toward a home for them because they believed it was the responsibility of the man's family to provide the marital home. Yet there was not a single case in my entire sample of 283 people where a man's parents did not help him buy a home because they believed it was the woman's responsibility to provide the marital home.

This pattern of parents favoring sons over daughters is troubling enough. Even more disturbing, though, is that many parents with an *only daughter* decline to help her make a down payment on a home specifically because she is female. One 23-year-old Shanghai resident, a university graduate and only daughter, said that she asked her parents to help her buy an apartment, but they resisted because they consider it shameful for her to own a home before marriage. "They don't want people to think I am a 'shrewd merchant' [*jingming shikuai*]," she says.

Another interviewee, a 26-year-old university-educated legal worker in Beijing and only daughter, said that her parents kept a detailed account of all the money they had spent on her over the years: for education, clothes, food, travel, extracurricular activities. They regularly showed her the itemized list of expenses to remind her that she owed them, and that they expected repayment. By contrast, not once did I hear of any parents demanding that their son repay them for helping him buy an expensive home, since parents often consider it their duty to do so. (Some of the sons I interviewed said they would feel bad if they didn't repay their parents later in life, but their parents pointedly did not expect repayment.)

In addition to declining to help their only daughter buy a home, some parents spend substantial sums — often in excess of RMB 100,000 or tens of thousands of US dollars — to buy a home for another male relative. I conducted in-depth interviews with seven women in Beijing and Shanghai who do not have brothers (six of whom are only children), and whose parents declined to help them buy a home, but helped a male relative buy one.

Yang Jin is a 27-year-old unmarried public relations manager and only child, living in Shanghai. "I have seriously considered buying a home of my own, but my conclusion is that I can't possibly afford it," says Yang. She asked her parents to help her buy a home, but they declined, even though in 2011 they and her two aunts gave more than RMB 200,000 (over US$31,000 then) to her male cousin on her mother's side in Guangzhou for a down payment on a home in his name. Yang says her cousin's wife also contributed financially to the home purchase, but Yang's mother and two aunts opposed adding the wife's name to the deed because her financial contribution was less than theirs. I asked Yang whether she would favour putting her name on a property deed if she marries and buys a house with her husband. "If my husband said that this house was mainly paid for by him and his family, I would certainly not ask to add my name," she replied.

Urban home ownership has become such a defining feature of masculinity that well-educated men who cannot afford to buy a home may feel a sense of shame or failure. Zhang Yin is a 27-year-old university graduate and Communist Party member who sells medical equipment to veterinary hospitals in Beijing. He earns a relatively high income (plus commission) of between RMB 10,000 and RMB 15,000 a month, which is more than twice – and sometimes more than three times – the average monthly wage in Beijing of RMB 4,672 (US$730) a month, according to the China Daily, based on NBS figures for 2011. Zhang works regular overtime so that he can save up enough money in the coming years to buy a home in Beijing. Asked if he would find it acceptable to rent rather than own his home, he responded:

> This is our culture; a home is a necessity [*bixupin*] … I couldn't possibly accept a life without owning a home. If my life turns out that way, then I would consider myself a big failure.

Zhang Yin's household registration or *hukou* is in Hebei province, so according to 2011 government regulations restricting the purchase of property in Beijing he must prove that he has worked in the city for five years (he moved there in 2009) in order to qualify to buy a Beijing home.

While many educated migrants to Beijing with sufficient money for a deposit were able to buy an apartment in the city prior to 2011 without a Beijing *hukou*, such people now have to wait at least five years before buying. As the CEO of a prominent Beijing property consultancy, Li Guoping, explained:

> This *gang xu* [strong demand] real estate market [which relies heavily on sales to those getting married or having children] has been clearly defined by the government. The government has placed other people outside the circle. Only people on the inside can play the game.

In this respect, aspiring homeowners who may be privileged on account of income or education are prevented from "playing the game" of property ownership because they lack the correct *hukou*, or have no financial backing from their family (a problem especially acute for women). A case in point: since medical equipment salesman Zhang Yin does not have a Beijing *hukou*, he must wait years to buy an urban home. He has often discussed home buying with his girlfriend, whom he hopes to marry in the next few years. They have agreed that if, after the five-year waiting period, they still cannot afford a home in Beijing, they will not have a child. Zhang says his income is higher than that of all his peers in Beijing, but he does not consider himself a success. "Without a home, I'm not a member of the middle class, I'm part of the lower class [*dichan jieji*]," says Zhang. After my interview with Zhang on a late Sunday morning, he said he had to go to work. I said to him *xinku le*, a polite phrase meaning that he works very hard. He replied: "Everyone works very hard [*dajia xinku*], in order to buy a home."

Zhang's single-minded perseverance and hard work to save enough money to buy a home is not unusual for an educated person in his or her mid- to late twenties. If their elders cannot afford to help them buy a home, young urban men and women often take upon themselves the crushing burden of having to save up enough money to make a down payment of up to several hundred thousand renminbi on the "necessity" (*bixupin*) of owning a small apartment in the city, which they view as the foundation for starting a family. The term *fangnu* – "house slave" – is widely used slang to refer to a homeowner who is tied down by expensive mortgage payments. Yet it is precisely the dream of many urban Chinese in their mid-twenties through their thirties to become a homeowner.

Note that even though Zhang's lack of a Beijing *hukou* shuts him out of urban home ownership for at least five years under current government regulations, he is still much better off than his sister and his girlfriend/future wife, simply because he is male. His parents already gave him and his brother land and houses in their own names in rural Hebei province, but they did not help their sister acquire land or build a home because she is female. Zhang says the gendered division of property is simply "Chinese tradition." He adds that if he and his future wife succeed in buying an urban home, he plans to put only his name on the deed.

While the state media narrative in outlets such as the flagship Communist Party publication *People's Daily* is that the tremendous pressure to buy an urban home falls solely on the shoulders of men, my findings demonstrate that women, too, experience great pressure to buy a home upon marriage. But whereas the men by and large wind up owning valuable real-estate wealth (as long as they have parents, girlfriends, wives, or other relatives to help them with the purchase), the pressure on *women* to buy a home often ends up with them paying hefty sums of money to finance it, but forfeiting their right to ownership.

When Chinese masculinity is defined in part by home ownership, women who are able to buy their own homes sometimes scare off potential husbands. A 31-year-old advertising manager in Xi'an, Lan Zheng, told me in 2012, "I really need a home of my own so that I can have a feeling of security [*anquan gan*]." She spoke very warmly about her fiancé, who was two years younger than her and admired her career success and strong sense of self. Yet in 2013, Lan sent me a long, distraught message saying that her fiancé had abruptly cancelled their upcoming wedding – under pressure from his parents – after she had purchased a small apartment in her own name in 2012. Although I did not interview her fiancé to hear his side of the story, Lan believes the fact that she bought the apartment in her own name played a major role in the break-up. Home prices in Xi'an, a second-tier city, are much more affordable than in the first-tier cities, and Lan paid a total of just RMB 150,000 (US$24,000 that year) for her sharply discounted apartment. What is particularly ironic about Lan's situation is that one of the reasons why she was so determined to buy a home of her own is that her rural parents had long ago built a home for her brother but not for her or her sister, because they are female.

Lesbians who say they never want to marry a man not surprisingly also have trouble convincing their parents to help them buy a home. Liu Yan is a 22-year-old lesbian in her last year at a prestigious university in Beijing. An only child, Liu is determined to buy a home of her own so that she can be independent. When she was 21 years old, she came out to her parents in Changchun – a city in China's north-east, much less progressive in its social values than cosmopolitan Beijing or Shanghai – and communicated her desire to buy a home. Since then, Liu's mother has often suggested that she consider marrying a man who is "economically strong" so that he can "take care of her." Liu's parents declined to help her to buy a home, even though in 2010 they gave her uncle RMB 100,000 (almost US$15,000 then) for his home purchase.

Gay men are often able to gain parental support for buying a home simply because they are male, but they, too, may be shut out of property ownership because they do not fit into the heterosexual pattern of marital home buying in urban China. (Gay marriage is not legal in China.) Take Fei Tong, a 29-year-old gay man and Ph.D. candidate in engineering in Beijing, who has not come out about his sexual orientation. Fei's parents gave him RMB 100,000 to help him buy a home in 2012. Fei then gave the money to his boyfriend to buy a home in his boyfriend's name only. Fei is living with his boyfriend in the home and contributing to mortgage payments; he tells his parents that his boyfriend is just his "roommate", and that he is still looking for the right home to purchase. "I cheated my parents out of the money for the home," says Fei, admitting that he feels guilty for not telling his parents about being gay and about having spent the money already. But Fei fears his parents won't understand him and that he will have trouble finding a job if he admits that he is gay. (See Chapter 6 for more on the LGBTQ community.)

Much more research needs to be done on how the new norm of buying a home upon getting married in China affects the LGBTQ community. I believe, however, that as long as the government continues to impose tight restrictions on buying residential real estate, the problem of *tongqi* – straight women marrying gay men, usually unwittingly – may worsen. Not only is there intense pressure on gays and lesbians to maintain the appearance of a heterosexual marriage, but government restrictions on buying property are making it increasingly difficult for a single person – of any sexual orientation – to buy a home.

Before mid-2012, for example, all migrants to Shanghai were free to buy a home so long as they had worked in the city for a year and could provide official tax receipts for their employment. Several young single women I interviewed in Shanghai in early 2012 expressed a strong desire to save up enough money to buy an apartment of their own, because under government regulations at the time they were allowed to become home owners even though they did not have a Shanghai household registration or *hukou*. But, in yet another act of official marriage promotion, the Shanghai government now allows only migrants who are *married* to buy a home. New government regulations introduced in mid-2012 make it impossible for single residents in Shanghai without a *hukou* to buy a home, no matter how long they have worked there. (Single people with a Shanghai *hukou* are now limited to buying just one apartment.)

The 2012 Shanghai regulations prohibiting single people without a *hukou* from buying a home therefore greatly increase the pressure on straight women and men to marry, but also on the LGBTQ community to fake a heterosexual marriage just for the sake of buying a home. Consider how easy it is for a young woman in her twenties, with little to no dating or sexual experience, to end up marrying a man who is gay. Some of the married women I interviewed had never had a romantic relationship with the man they agreed to marry.

Shanghai resident Zhang Jie is 25 and recently married. She had never dated anyone while studying for her B.A. degree in engineering at one of China's top universities. Her parents had always encouraged her to focus on her education since she was their only child, and they did not want her to be to be distracted by romance. Upon graduation, Zhang landed a plum job at a multinational consulting company, then worked hard to get promoted; she is already making around RMB 10,000 (around US$1,600) a month, well above the average income in Shanghai (RMB 4,331 a month in 2011, according to *China Daily*). One day, a colleague eleven years her senior asked Zhang if she would like to get married and buy a home together.

"At my age, it's definitely not too early to get married, so I said yes," says Zhang. At first, her parents were concerned about the fact that her prospective husband was so much older than their daughter (he is 36); that his rural parents had very little education (they never graduated from high school, but Zhang thinks that they know how to read and write); and that, despite his age, his salary was no higher than hers. But they quickly came around. After all, Zhang was already 25; she and her parents agreed that if she did not jump at the chance to get married now, she might become a "leftover" woman.

When the couple got engaged, Zhang visited her fiancé's parents, who are farmers in Liaoning province, north-eastern China. Their son had never brought a girlfriend home before. After years of worrying that he would never marry, they were ecstatic to find out that he would be marrying such a well-educated, accomplished woman from the big city.

Six months after they obtained their marriage registration, Zhang and her husband were making mortgage payments on a marital home that cost almost RMB 2 million (US$330,000). Zhang used her savings of roughly RMB 100,000 (around US$16,000) to make the initial payment on the essential fittings required to turn the "naked" concrete shell of an apartment into a habitable home. The couple have never had sex, however. Zhang explained that since the home fittings are not yet finished, she continued to live with her parents, while her husband rented an apartment with his male university classmate.

"I'm rather conservative, and I think it's better if we wait to sleep together – and my parents agree," she says. Her husband never pressed the issue of having sex with her and, according to her, doesn't think it is important. She says they will sleep together once they move into their new home, but adds: "My husband also recognizes that we should each have separate bedrooms." Has Zhang ever thought about staying overnight at her husband's rented apartment? No, because that would be inconvenient (*mafan*). "My husband's apartment is tiny, and he shares a bedroom with his classmate."

This scenario does not strike Zhang as strange. She did not think to go on a few romantic dates with her husband – or with anyone else – before she agreed to marry. Yet she did not hesitate to enter into a complicated financial transaction with him involving the purchase of expensive real estate, the ramifications of which could stay with her for the rest of her life.

Zhang says that she is heterosexual, so from her point of view the marriage is not just one of convenience. But she did not want her husband to know that she was taking part in my research project, so I did not meet him. During our two-hour interview, I didn't have the heart to ask Zhang if she has considered the possibility that her husband might actually be gay. I couldn't help but recall that in China today at least 10 million straight women are married to gay men, according to a leading expert on LGBT issues, Zhang Beichuan, who found that nearly 90 percent of gay men in China are married to or will marry heterosexual women in order to fend off family and social pressure. (See Chapter 6 for more on lesbians and marriage.)

How state promotion of marriage and new households fuels real-estate mania

For China's previous generation, housing was a benefit heavily subsidized by the state. After the 1949 Communist Revolution, the Chinese government nationalized private housing and allocated public housing through work units. The government controlled all land transactions, most urban land was state-owned, and rent was extremely low. In 1980, paramount leader Deng Xiaoping announced a change in urban housing policy, which led to reform experiments. From 1993 to 1997, the government allowed private companies to participate in housing development; and in 1998, the State Council terminated welfare-based housing allocation to set up a market-based system of home ownership. Nevertheless, housing remains an important vestige of socialist-era entitlements. Sociologist Ching Kwan Lee writes that rural land rights and urban home ownership are "forms of state redistribution that cushion workers from destitution and dispossession caused by market competition."

Many studies document that urban homes in China are now "severely unaffordable" according to price-to-income ratios. A 2012 survey of the four "first-tier" cities of Beijing, Shanghai, Guangzhou, and Shenzhen conducted by Horizon China found that the average home cost over fifteen times the buyer's annual income, while over a third of buyers said their home cost more than twenty times their annual income. By another measure, an average home in Beijing cost more than twenty-two times the buyer's annual income, whereas the median house price in New York – one of the most expensive cities in the United States for buying property – was equal to 6.2 years' worth of the median pretax household income in 2011, according to International Monetary Fund (IMF) analysis of data from Euromoney Institutional Investor Company (CEIC) and the 8th Annual Demographia International Housing Affordability Survey.

Yet, as noted before, China has one of the highest home ownership rates in the world, with 85 percent urban home ownership, according to China's central bank. Sociologist Sun Liping writes that China's residential property prices are high because three households (the marital couple and both sets of parents) pay for one home. The heavy parental support for home buying also partly explains why first-time homebuyers in cities like Beijing are only around 27 years old. Property ownership has become a particularly important marker of Chinese middle-class identity, with many high-income earners living in "high-class neighborhoods" (*gaodang xiaoqu*).

These dynamics have emerged only within the last decade, ever since China's real-estate boom took off and urban home prices experienced double-digit growth rates starting in the mid-2000s. In today's China, urban men and women in their mid-twenties to early thirties often aspire to purchase a home shortly before or after marriage, although this is an unaffordable dream for many. Real-estate sales professionals use the term "strong demand" (*gang xu*) to describe the sector of middle-class consumers who have propelled most residential property sales since the imposition of new government property controls. According to sales professionals, *gang xu* demand comes largely from urban consumers experiencing the following life events: (1) marriage; (2) pregnancy and birth of the first child; (3) a child starting school.

Of the hundreds of people in their twenties to mid-thirties who participated in this survey, only a small number (such as some government officials who are guaranteed housing for life at very low rates) say that they have no desire to buy a home. The social norm of buying a home shortly before or after marriage is so strong that a couple getting married without first buying a home are said to have a "naked marriage" (*luohun*). Many respondents say that it is "Chinese culture" which fuels the seemingly insatiable demand for homes, despite their severe unaffordability. Yet the demand for homes among middle-class Chinese consumers (as opposed to speculators) is to a large extent the result of successful marketing strategies on the part of property developers and matchmaking companies, combined with state media reports and new state policies restricting property purchases. These state and private business interests intertwine to create and promote the myth that buying a home is a necessity for middle-class Chinese starting a family. Moreover, China's financial services industry is still at a nascent stage, and most consumers have nowhere else to invest their money other than in residential property.

Sociologist Pierre Bourdieu, in *The Social Structures of the Economy*, described the market in single-family houses as a "*twofold social construction* to which the state contributes crucially: the [social] construction of demand, through the production of individual dispositions" and the "[social] construction of supply, through the policy of the state (or the banks)." Bourdieu's interpretation of the housing market as the social construction of demand and supply is especially true for China. The Chinese state controls the supply of residential real estate through its invasive regulations on property purchases, with nationwide property purchase restrictions announced in 2010, and new local restrictions continually being announced, such as requiring buyers to make higher down payments, restricting home purchases to residents with an urban *hukou* or to residents who are married. Property consultant Li Guoping describes government property controls (*tiaokong*) as an economic form of stability maintenance (*weiwen*), an "economic lever" to prevent the real-estate market and economy from collapsing:

> Everyone – from regional governments to the central government
> – depends on playing the real estate game. How do you play?
> You can't let it get too hot. If you marketize [fully], speculators
> would certainly make all the money, the property market would
> be in trouble, and the economy would collapse. And with China's
> economic structural system now, the system wouldn't be able to
> survive a collapse of the real estate market, unlike the US, which

was able to absorb it... So the government will not dare to remove property controls [*tiaokong*] for the next couple of years. Stability maintenance [*weiwen*] is the core of China's politics – including *weiwen* in the economy and *weiwen* in the property market.

The property controls imposed by the state restrain speculative investment in China's prime real-estate markets, but the government does not want demand for residential property among middle-class consumers to collapse either. Therefore, the state also controls the supply of residential real estate through large, state-owned property development companies, which have an enormous influence over the country's real-estate market.

One Beijing-based sales manager for a state-owned property development company told me that since the imposition of new purchase restrictions in 2011, the company has not sold as many apartments as it used to. But, despite the weaker demand for property, he says that "we can never lower the price of apartments, because people who bought homes in the past will get very upset." Isolated homeowner protests over falling property prices have taken place since government property controls were tightened, such as a group of 400 Shanghai homeowners trashing the showroom of one of China's top real-estate developers, Longfor Properties. The company's Beijing manager said in 2012 that his operation had already "reached its sales quota" for that year, and that rather than attempting to sell more apartments by lowering prices, it would simply not sponsor any more large sales events until the next year.

In another example of the state keeping property prices artificially high, in 2008 Zhou Jiugeng, head of the land bureau of Nanjing, said he would punish real-estate developers who dared to sell their houses below cost price. Zhou was subsequently sentenced to a prison term for bribery. Nevertheless state-owned property development companies still do not cut their prices. They are able to keep property prices high because they benefit from elite government clients and access to much cheaper credit than private property developers.

China's Central Propaganda Bureau and State Council Information Office issued directives to the state media that "regarding regulation and control of the real-estate market, all websites must successfully lead public opinion and propaganda... They must actively promote [efforts by] the Chinese Communist Party and State Council to resolutely restrain rapid increases in real-estate prices," according to documents obtained by *China Digital Times*. The leaked directives instruct Chinese state media to avoid the "politically sensitive" topic of housing prices: "Resolutely execute public opinion guidance on the real-estate market. Do not conduct questionnaires or online surveys on housing prices."

The state wants to keep speculators from causing the property market to overheat and collapse, but it does not want existing property prices to fall significantly, so it constructs the notion of "strong demand" (*gang xu*) for real estate among middle-class consumers – focusing on young men and women getting married and having children. According to many economists, the formation of new households is a key driver of economic growth. Moody's Analytics estimated in 2011 that each new household formed in the United States "adds about US$145,000 to output each year" as its spending moves through the economy. It stands to reason, then, that the Chinese state has an incentive to promote the formation of new households and housing sales associated with marriage and the birth of children. The economic benefits of new household formation dovetail with the demographic benefits of promoting marriage for urban educated women through the "leftover" women media campaign.

Chinese state media may be prohibited from discussing housing prices in detail, but they publish frequent surveys and features on marriage and housing, which help generate the desire among young men and women for residential real estate. The media, property developers, and the matchmaking industry construct demand among the "post-'80" and "post-'90" generation (those born after 1980 and 1990 respectively) through online surveys on attitudes to love and marriage, which are linked to real-estate advertising. For example, Sina Property Sales (the same company that runs Weibo) and the matchmaking company Baihe.com conducted a large-scale online survey in early 2012, "Young People's Attitudes to Marital Housing," asking Weibo users to vote on whether it is better to buy a home before or after marriage, and whether a woman is willing to marry a man if he does not already own a home.

In considering the Chinese obsession with home buying, sometimes it can be difficult to distinguish the desires of the younger generation from the exhortations of the parents. Young women and men in China continue to feel a deep sense of filial piety and obligation to the family, to the degree that some people in their twenties or thirties say they would not feel so anxious about buying a home were it not for pressure from their parents or other elders. On the other hand, many young people say that they want to buy a home because they want the security that they believe will come with home ownership:

> I can accept a "naked marriage" [*luohun*, getting married without buying a home], but I need to own a home before I have a child... If I don't own a home, I won't have a safeguard [*baozhang*]. I can't get sick or travel or take a break from working.
>
> 28-year-old man with a college degree, Beijing

> I want to buy a home in my own name, even if I get married, so that I can have a sense of security [*anquan gan*].
>
> 27-year-old woman with a college degree, Shanghai

I have encountered very few Chinese college graduates in their late twenties who do not worry about buying a home (if their relatives have not already given them one). Many of these young people consider home ownership to be a prerequisite for a sense of belonging to the middle class. This psychological and financial burden stands in striking contrast to Americans in their late twenties, who in the past few decades have become *less* interested in assuming the financial burden of buying a home. Economists Jonas Fisher and Martin Gervais's 2011 paper, "Why Has Home Ownership Fallen among the Young?" documents a sharp decline in home ownership among young American "household heads" aged between 25 and 44 from 1980 to 2000, long before the US housing market collapse of 2006. They attribute this decline largely to delayed marriage and worries about economic insecurity.

It is possible that if China had a comprehensive social security system, young Chinese would no longer feel the need to buy a home to achieve a sense of economic security. Many want a home as an investment, because there is no other viable place to invest their money. Many say that if they had more rights as renters, they would be less anxious to buy a home. Even men and women in their mid-twenties say they do not like the possibility of having to move if their landlord decides to sell their apartment or rent it to someone else, and indeed renters are regularly evicted from their apartments. Many consumers who do not have a *hukou* household registration in the city wish to buy a home so that they can obtain more *hukou*-related rights, such as their future child being allowed to attend school, or receiving heavily subsidized healthcare.

Nobel prize-winning economist Amartya Sen might characterize the perspectives of non-homeowning Chinese as a form of inequality based on being deprived of perceived community needs:"For example, being relatively poor in a rich community can prevent a person from achieving some elementary functionings (such as taking part in the life of the community) even though her income, in absolute terms, may be much higher than the level of income at which members of poorer communities can function with great ease and success."

Contrast the predicament of educated, relatively high-income women (and sometimes men) who cannot afford to buy a home with that of 28-year-old Deng Xin, a male university graduate with a Beijing *hukou*, who is also a Communist Party member. Deng's parents made a down payment of almost RMB 300,000 (almost US$48,000) on an RMB 800,000 (almost US$130,000) home in his name in August 2012. After his parents had paid the deposit, Deng began to make mortgage payments of roughly RMB 3,500 (US$560) a month, half the monthly income of some RMB 7,000 (US$1,100) he makes as an online news editor. Deng is single. He says that if he marries and has a child, he will need to buy another home that is larger than his current property of 68 square meters. Even though Deng's income is significantly less than that of other urban residents in their late twenties, the fact that he owns residential real estate places him, by his own standards, within the Chinese middle class.

Feelings of anxiety and frustration are common for educated urban women and men in their late twenties to early thirties whose families do not help them buy a home. Yet this frustration over unaffordable home prices does not, as yet, appear to be leading to social action. In *Myth of the Social Volcano*, sociologist Martin King Whyte writes that most Chinese survey respondents "voiced more acceptance than anger about current inequalities." Sociologist Ching Kwan Lee also concludes that even though many Chinese condemn injustice, they still believe that "inequality is inevitable or historically necessary." Young Chinese in their twenties and early thirties seem, by and large, to accept that they must work extremely hard in order to save up enough money to make the down payment on a home. Currently, very few of China's younger generation vow to opt out of the norm of home-buying. Rather than being the source of new social conflict, the widespread perception of home ownership as a precondition of middle-class entry appears to have simply made young women and men even more obsessed with saving money to buy a home.

The Chinese state has apparently imposed new controls on buying property not just to prevent prices from rising too high as a result of speculative investment, but also to ensure that prices do not fall too much. Demand for residential real estate is kept high in numerous ways: state-owned property development companies do not lower their prices significantly; property development companies collaborate with state media and the matchmaking industry to reinforce the norm that couples need to buy a home when they get married; state media and real-estate advertisements perpetuate the myth that Chinese women will refuse to marry a man unless he owns a home; and new regulations on property purchases in cities, such as Shanghai, discriminate against unmarried home buyers.

It is possible that in addition to developing policies to maintain political stability, the Chinese state wants to ensure that property prices remain sufficiently high that most aspiring, middle-class home buyers must work so hard to save money to become a household that they have no desire to concern themselves with deeper political questions. Middle-class activism tends to revolve around "not-in-my-back-yard" (NIMBY) environmental concerns, such as protesting the construction of a chemical plant which might pollute the neighborhood; or it involves homeowner associations unhappy with the management of their residential compounds. But middle-class activism among homeowners has yet to demonstrate any serious potential for collective action that challenges central government rule. Sociologist Jean-Louis Rocca explains in his analysis of Chinese homeowners and the political behavior of the middle class:

> From the homeowners' point of view, the Central Government is on the right side of the picture. "Our leaders are good, no problem, the direction given is right" sums up the general attitude of the people I interviewed... The line between participation in movements and political protests is never crossed. Of course, it is possible that this is for tactical reasons: political demands could lead to a breakdown in the negotiations with the authorities. However, it is also clearly linked to the fact that homeowners usually consider entering the political field to be dangerous – dangerous for them, but also for Chinese society. "China does not need a change in political regime. It needs stability."

Just as the existing urban propertied class tends to support the one-party state and the "stability" it brings, so aspiring home buyers in their twenties and early thirties tend not to voice opposition to the central government. The pursuit of money for a deposit on a new home saps much of their time and energy.

Many have written about how China's youth are apathetic about politics. Chinese in their twenties through to early thirties, also known as the "post-'80 generation" (*balinghou*, born after 1980), are seen as very pragmatic and materialistic, focused on their own private lives, unwilling to risk their economic upward mobility by engaging in political debates. Would China's youth be more politically engaged if they weren't pressured into marrying and buying a home so early in life, in most cases almost as soon as they graduate from college or a master's program?

Most young Chinese recognize the sharp inequality in society, but – for now – they also want to join rather than overthrow the privileged, propertied class. Homes are unaffordable, but nevertheless not so expensive that educated young Chinese abandon hope of ever being able to buy – especially when, in most cases, their parents or elders provide significant financial help. My research suggests that, rather than *causing* political instability, high property prices and the norm of middle-class home ownership might actually *promote* social stability by forcing young Chinese to focus on saving money to buy into the propertied class rather than agitating for social change.

Why real-estate wealth is more important than income for Chinese women

It is essential to understand the role of the residential real-estate market in fueling China's rapidly growing wealth inequality, particularly along gender lines. The severe unaffordability of homes in China means that it is now virtually impossible for one young person alone to make the down payment on a new home in a first-tier city, and extremely difficult in a second-tier or even third-tier city. No matter how high their income, most young people cannot buy a home if their parents or other family members are unable or unwilling to provide heavy financing for them, according to my own research and the 2012 survey by Horizon China of thousands of home buyers in Beijing, Shanghai, Guangzhou, and Shenzhen.

The norm of male home ownership means that assets in the family largely flow toward men, because men are seen to have a strong need for a home of their own, while women are seen as not needing independent home ownership. When assets are pooled, the parents and other elders who have contributed money to a deposit have undue power of influence over whose name should be registered on the property deed. Since relatives tend to contribute more money toward buying a home for a man, even when a woman getting married contributes a substantial amount of money to the down payment, the sum tends to be less than the amount contributed by the man's family. This is just one of many factors that explain why the man's family tends to win in the negotiation over whose name goes on the deed.

What is astonishing is that these large family wealth transfers – a living form of inheritance – are made without being subject to any taxes. At the time of writing, China has yet to pass a national law on property tax or inheritance tax to prevent the excessive concentration of wealth in the hands of the few. This creation of wealth inequality through family transfers of property assets is potentially even more extreme than in the United States – a country notable for its high level of inequality – where estate, gift and property taxes are imposed.

The unprecedented accumulation of over US$30 trillion in residential real-estate wealth in the hands of some Chinese and not others is certainly a factor in the country's widening wealth gap, which many studies indicate is now larger than in the United States and in some African countries. Li Gan, director of the Survey and Research Center for China Household Finance in Chengdu (and an economist at Texas A&M University in the United States) recently conducted a comprehensive study of household wealth in China. In Professor Li's 2013 update of the study, he found that the top 10 percent of Chinese households had garnered 85 percent of total assets and 57 percent of total income. Li also finds that the mean nominal gain in first-home value is 340 percent. Real estate is the largest source of wealth for the super-rich in cities such as Shanghai, according to the Chinese Millionaire Wealth Report published annually by the Hurun Report, a luxury publishing and events group in Shanghai.

The creation of this stark new form of gender inequality in wealth has profound and long-lasting consequences for China beyond the mere question of who will get the marital home in the event of divorce. Many scholars have argued that the distribution of wealth through assets (such as private property) is much more important than income distribution as a measure of socioeconomic well-being. Sociologist Yuval Elmelech explains in his *Transmitting Inequality: Wealth and the American Family* that the most important form of wealth often depends on family transfers of assets:

> *Stock* of material resources (private property, net worth) has precedence over *flow* of material resources (income, earnings). As such, wealth inequality is critical not only to an understanding of economic disparity, but also to the distribution and replication of power and status. ... [F]*amily-based transactions* of material resources are important mechanisms that determine position in the stratification system.

Many economic studies of the racial wealth gap in the United States also demonstrate that inheritances, bequests, and intra-family wealth transfers are more important than other indicators such as education or income in perpetuating entrenched socioeconomic inequality. Economists Darrick Hamilton and William Darity Jr. write that "intra-familial transfers, the primary source of wealth for most Americans with positive net worth, are transfers of blatant non-merit resources."

While intra-family asset transfers are important in American wealth accumulation, these transfers of "blatant, non-merit resources" appear to be even more critical in post-socialist China, where there is no tax on inheritance or family gift-giving (at the time of writing). In China, studies show that, on account of the lack of other viable investment alternatives, residential real estate is the most important asset for most households. Women are obviously not the only members of society to be hurt by China's skyrocketing home prices. Nevertheless those who have succeeded in buying an urban home are largely men. For these male homeowners, real-estate wealth becomes what Pierre Bourdieu calls "the central element in a patrimony," which influences class, status, and power and is likely to be passed on completely tax-free to the next generation.

Compared with all the Chinese women who are shut out of valuable real-estate wealth in one way or another, consider how much freedom and independence a woman gains when she has a home in her own name. Shang Wen is a 30-year-old Beijing resident and only daughter with a 1-year-old boy. She stands out from most people in China because she pursued her undergraduate studies in Great Britain. When she graduated and moved to Beijing in 2004, her parents paid the deposit on a home for her, in her name. "Real estate was not too expensive then, and my parents had no idea the market was going to take off," says Shang. Since she bought at the very beginning of the real-estate boom in Beijing, her two-bedroom apartment in central Beijing cost a total of just RMB 950,000 (US$114,000 in 2004), and the down payment was only 20 percent. The minimum deposit required for a first-time purchase of a Beijing home is now 30 percent (in 2013), and home prices have soared over the past decade.

Shang could afford mortgage payments of RMB 5,000 per month on account of her high-paying job at an international media company. Shang married just a few months after meeting her husband at the end of 2010, because she had reached the "leftover" woman age threshold and all her friends were getting married and having babies. "I was getting older and older and there was this pressure; it's stupid, but it exists," she says now. Her husband was a doctor at a state hospital who earned much less than she did, but his relatively low income did not deter her. Shang's mother expressed some doubts about his character, but did not try to dissuade her daughter from marrying him.

As soon as the couple were engaged, the man moved into Shang's apartment. But they started fighting the very night that they obtained their marriage registration and this continued, even after Shang got pregnant. The relationship deteriorated further after she gave birth to her son. "My husband refused to help with any of the housework, but the last straw was that he didn't care about the baby," said Shang. At the end of 2012, she divorced her husband after he became violent and hit her father, giving him a black eye. Since Shang's home was registered solely in her name, she was able to ask her husband to move out and the court allowed her to claim the home. Now that Shang is divorced she is much happier; her parents help take care of her son.

Shang's story validates the conclusion of many studies: when women have their own source of wealth independent of the marriage, their bargaining power within the marriage increases, and their well-being after divorce is much greater than that of women who lack wealth of their own. Studies also show that wealth through assets is a far better indicator of economic well-being than income, which is dependent on employment and can ebb and flow. My own research suggests that in China, *home ownership* in itself is much more significant than income alone as a source of wealth and power both within the marriage and in the event of divorce. Women who own a home have economic power that can translate into greater freedom in many other areas of their lives.

Yet the majority of women in China are not as lucky as Shang Wen. When women do not have ownership of their own home, the consequences can be dire, especially if they have an abusive husband. The next chapter examines how Chinese women's property rights have changed over time, how historical traditions have contributed to the low status of women, and why gender inequality has been so difficult to eradicate in today's China.

FOUR

Back to the Ming dynasty

Ding Shen exudes confidence as she relates her home-buying aspirations over an after-work dinner in Shanghai.

"I don't care if the man I marry has a home, but I want to buy a home all of my own, with my name on the deed," says Ding, a single, IT sales manager, 27 years old at the time of my first interview with her in 2012. "Even if I'm married, I still want a separate home in my name," says Ding, laughing out loud. "There are always bumpy times in life, and if I'm unhappy in the relationship, I want a place to escape to."

Ding has worked in Shanghai ever since she graduated from university. Her mother pressures her to marry, but she is not in a rush. "In my Ma's way of thinking, I'm already an old maid [*da guniang*]," she says, laughing broadly. "But I feel I'm still very young; I can still enjoy the single life for a few more years… After you marry, you're often just leading a deathly life [*si shenghuo*]. I don't want to be controlled by someone else. I want to be in control of my own life."

Yet Ding's strong desire for economic independence and personal freedom clashes with the traditional values of her parents. Ding is the eldest of three daughters and her parents have a rural *hukou*, or household registration, in the central Chinese province of Henan. (Although she was born after China imposed its one-child policy, the policy was often only loosely enforced in the countryside, where a couple who gave birth to a girl were generally allowed to try again for a boy. China announced an official loosening of the policy in November 2013, allowing couples to have two children if one of the parents is an only child.) Not only are Ding's parents anxious about her casual approach to marriage; they have also declined to make even a small contribution to her savings for a down payment on a home. They also declined to help any of their other daughters financially. It's not that her parents are too poor to give any money to their daughters; they simply believe that their nephew's claim to their money takes precedence over the claims of their daughters, because he is the man in the family. Two years earlier, they gave tens of thousands of RMB to Ding's older, male cousin (*biaoge*) to help him buy a home – in cash, leaving no mortgage debt – in Henan province. Meanwhile, Ding saves as much of her own income as she can, hoping that perhaps one day she might be able to make enough money to put down a deposit on her own home.

Does Ding feel a sense of injustice? No, she insists, explaining matter-of-factly that this is the way her parents view the world. "My parents have no obligation to help me buy a home, but my *biaoge* has nowhere to live," she says.

Had Ding lived a thousand years earlier in China's Song dynasty (960–1279), she might have stood a better chance of acquiring property in her own name.

The golden age for women's property rights: 1,000 years ago?

During the Song dynasty, women had substantial, independent ownership and control of property, according to historian Bettine

Birge's *Women, Property and Confucian Reaction in Sung and Yuan China (960–1368)*:

> More property was transferred to women than at any time
> previously in Chinese history. Most strikingly, traditional law
> that was originally meant to keep inheritance along the … male
> line was reinterpreted to allow considerable assets to pass out of
> the patriline [through sons] to daughters. Other laws protected
> a woman's property within marriage and allowed her to take
> all of it into a remarriage in the case of widowhood or divorce.
> These developments gave elite women unprecedented economic
> independence…

It wasn't just elite women who enjoyed strong rights to property in the Song dynasty; most of the women (and men) studied by Birge held property to some degree:

> Often they owned only small amounts of land or occasionally only
> movable property. They appeared on the government registers as
> members of taxable households, and while they might not have
> been well off, they were not people of servile status. This group
> represented a majority of the population, not just the elite…
> Property and related social standing were major sources of agency
> for women.

Historian Kathryn Bernhardt writes in *Women and Property in China, 960–1949* that, contrary to conventional wisdom, women's property rights ebbed and flowed throughout imperial Chinese history. The imperial tradition of patrilineal succession meant that a father's property was generally equally divided among sons. Yet in about one in five families, no sons survived to adulthood. Up to one-third of women were either daughters without brothers or wives without sons – or both – according to Bernhardt, and in these cases patrilineal succession became more complicated. Women's increased rights to property in the Song dynasty had the greatest effect in "extinct households," *juehu* or *hujue* – that is, "households that had died out for the lack of a male heir" – so that daughters were permitted to inherit property if the parents died without a son. "It is these women, as daughters and wives in the absence of men, who bring out in sharpest relief the different implications of patrilineal succession," writes Bernhardt.

Bettine Birge argues that the expansion of women's property rights in the Song dynasty included women who had brothers as well. She finds a "mountain" of evidence to show that during the Song dynasty the state supported inheritance of property by daughters even in the presence of sons, a practice that countered Confucian norms of inheritance along male lines only: "References to 'daughters' portions' (nü-fen 女分) are numerous; and they are found in different places and across centuries. The frequent mention of laws and lawsuits further confirms that daughters (and their husbands) might have recourse to the state if these portions were not distributed fairly."

Here, it is worth repeating that almost *one thousand years later*, in 2010, a nationwide survey conducted by the Women's Federation and NBS showed that only one out of fifteen single women in China owned a home in their own right. More comparative research needs to be done on the subject, but it appears that women in eleventh-century China may have had greater property rights' protection than the women of today.

Whereas daughters in twenty-first-century China have no recourse when their parents favor their brothers or male cousins in acquiring property, Song dynasty law a thousand years earlier provided an extraordinary range of state support for women's property rights, including the preservation of assets for under-age girls as well as boys. Birge writes that Song laws demonstrated not just official protection for daughters' property ownership in their own right, but also "distrust of relatives." For example, Birge cites Northern Song dynasty statesman Ssu-ma Kuang (1019–1086), who describes an unmarried daughter suing her brothers to assert her entitlement to family property following the death of her father:

> When the man died, his sons fought over the property, and "even his virgin daughter veiled her head and clutching documents went to the prefectural court to sue for her dowry property." These examples confirm that daughters had certain inheritance rights based on the laws of "equal division." According to these laws, an orphaned daughter could sue to receive her fair share of family property.

Moreover, when in the Song dynasty women married, the law allowed them to keep their property indefinitely, including after divorce or widowhood. The special legal treatment of women's property by the Song state "transmitted unprecedented assets through daughters and gave women unforeseen economic independence and mobility within marriage and beyond," writes Birge.

At the same time, Confucian philosophers from the tenth through to the thirteenth century challenged women's rights to property, since property ownership by women conflicted with the Confucian norm of an unbroken line of male descendants to perform ritual duties of ancestral sacrifice, according to Birge. Confucianism underwent a revival in the Song dynasty, particularly in the form of *dao xue*, or the "Learning of the Way," which taught women to obey their fathers at home, their husbands after marriage, and their sons in old age. Yet, until the Mongol conquest of China and the establishment of the Yuan dynasty (around 1279), Confucian reformers failed to change the laws supporting women's control of property, records Birge.

Even though women experienced a substantial expansion of property rights in the Song dynasty, it is curious that this was also the time when painful practices of binding the feet of well-to-do young girls became widespread. Historian Dorothy Ko probes the multifaceted meanings of the Chinese practice of footbinding for women from the twelfth through to the twentieth century in *Cinderella's Sisters: A Revisionist History of Footbinding*. Bound feet were considered attractive to men, and a desirable feature for a young woman hoping to marry well. More historical research needs to be done on why women's property rights flourished in the Song dynasty at the same time that foot-binding practices were born, but that discussion is beyond the scope of this book.

The decisive turn against women's property rights occurred at the end of the Song dynasty and the beginning of the Yuan dynasty in the thirteenth century, when the Mongol invasion of China led to what Birge calls a "re-Confucianization of the law" and a reversal of the steady improvements in Chinese women's property rights made since the tenth century. The onset of the Yuan dynasty (1279–1368) marked the beginning of new inheritance practices that were in line with Mongol steppe traditions and with the new Yuan state's turn back to the patriarchal principles of Confucianism. After the Mongol conquest of the thirteenth century, daughters began to lose privileges they had enjoyed in the Song dynasty and widows were forced to leave their dowries behind when they remarried, giving husbands much greater power over their wives. Yuan dynasty laws and social norms regarding property, marriage, and reproduction were transformed to the detriment of women, observes Birge.

Women's property rights deteriorated even further during the Ming dynasty of 1368–1644, with the adoption of a law putting nephews before daughters and widows, according to Bernhardt. In 1369, the Hongwu emperor, the founder and first emperor of the Ming Dynasty, announced a new law stating that if families did not have a son, they were required to designate the nephew as the father's heir. "If a sonless man did not make a lineage nephew his heir during his lifetime, the emperor decreed, his widow must (*xu*) do so after his death. If she failed to establish an heir during her lifetime, then the man's surviving relatives must do so after her death," writes Bernhardt.

With the Ming dynasty adoption of the law on "mandatory nephew succession" (a term Bernhardt uses in her book), the property rights of daughters and widows contracted dramatically. Bernhardt explains:

> For a daughter, the adoption of mandatory nephew succession in the early Ming meant a virtual loss of any right to inherit in the absence of brothers. Simply put, whereas in the Song a daughter was legally entitled to inherit the family property should her parents die without any sons, whether biological or adopted, under the rule of nephew succession, the claims of nephews took precedence over her claims. A daughter's likelihood of inheriting property by default was very remote.

The new law also meant that widows were only permitted to have custody of the property until they adopted a "lineage nephew" as their husband's heir.

Bernhardt argues that the early Ming state adopted the laws of "mandatory nephew succession" because it needed male hereditary soldier households for the survival of its military system. Since around 20 percent of married men had no male heirs at that time, the Ming state would have lost most of its manpower within a few generations. A daughter in the Ming dynasty could therefore only inherit property if she lacked both brothers and male cousins. Women's property rights did not improve again until the following Qing dynasty (1644–1911), when laws were relaxed somewhat to allow widows and widowed concubines more authority over property. The Qing state granted widows the right to choose which nephew could inherit property in the absence of sons, Bernhardt observes.

In today's China, when some parents prefer to give money to their nephew rather than to their own daughter to buy a home, they are reverting back to the practice from the Ming dynasty, when, in the absence of sons, daughters had less of a claim to property than nephews. (See Chapter 3 for more on parents favoring sons and sometimes nephews over daughters in buying property.) The parents of Shanghai IT consultant Ding Shen may not be aware of the fourteenth-century law of "mandatory nephew succession." Yet the fact that they believe their nephew has a right to their money to build a home simply because he is male reflects how centuries-old discriminatory social customs can persist in remarkable ways and reappear in the twenty-first century. Moreover, Ding Shen herself did not question (at least openly) this assumption that her male cousin had a greater entitlement to a home than she did, even though she expressly stated a strong desire to buy her own home.

Throughout most of China's imperial history, citizens were expected to marry and have sons to continue the patriline. Historian Susan L. Mann writes in *Gender and Sexuality in Modern Chinese History* that there was a "historical imperative" requiring that women in respectable families be cloistered at home, concealed from public view. In upper-class families, girls were educated up to the age of 12 along with their brothers, but were then pulled into the "women's quarters," *guige*, where they were groomed for marriage, in part by learning wifely skills such as embroidery, sewing, or making tiny shoes to fit their bound feet. For the elite woman, marriage led to a contraction and confinement of her life, while for an elite man, marriage marked an important step toward furthering his public career. The intense pressure in China today for young women and men to marry has long historical roots.

China's sex ratio imbalance in the twenty-first century is also echoed in history, not just the result of modern, restrictive family planning policies. In the nineteenth century, almost 100 percent of women married, but up to 20 percent of men never did, according to Mann. Even after working for decades as servants, older women were still desirable marriage candidates in the mid-Qing dynasty because rich families acquired concubines, in part to improve their chances of having a child (in particular, a boy). But impoverished young men often died without ever marrying. Back in the nineteenth century, unmarried men without wives or children were called "bare branches" or *guanggun*, just as they are today. These men were closely monitored by the government and "perceived as disruptive, predatory, and undisciplined by the constraints of life in a settled family home," says Mann.

As in today's China, problems with the sex-ratio imbalance during the mid-Qing dynasty of the eighteenth and nineteenth centuries resulted from the neglect or infanticide of baby girls, since most married couples at the time preferred to have sons in order to produce a male heir for the patriline. Mann describes a sex and gender continuum of cloistered young women "surrounded by institutions and relationships that hold the social order in place" at one end, and the rootless young man, a "free-floating marginal figure whose presence is a continuing threat to that social order," at the other end.

Compare the mid-Qing dynasty concerns about "bare branches" with warnings from a 2012 *People's Daily* editorial that "the continual accumulation of unmarried men of legal marrying age greatly increases the risk of social instability," citing reports that unmarried men in villages threaten the social order through activities such as "gambling, rioting, stealing and gang fighting."

Since women had few property rights in the Qing dynasty (in contrast with the Song dynasty centuries earlier), women's bodies constituted a form of property which could be exchanged through marriage. Elaborate transactions and betrothal gifts accompanied the exchange of rights over the daughter through arranged marriage, since she was expected to move to the home of her husband's parents and take care of his household. The groom's family traditionally paid a betrothal gift involving jewelry, clothes, and cash as compensation to the bride's family for transferring rights to the bride. If the bride's family wanted to be seen as respectable, it would also provide the groom's family with a lavish dowry, which matched or sometimes exceeded the cost of betrothal gifts and wedding costs paid by the groom's family, according to Mann.

Women's "liberation" in the Republican and Communist revolutions

In the nineteenth and twentieth centuries, China was convulsed by political and military crises from outside and inside the country. In the Opium Wars of 1839–42 and 1856–60, the British Empire forced China to open up to trade and imported ideologies from outside. Internally, China faced the massive political and religious Taiping Rebellion of 1850–64, led by Hong Xiuquan, a man who believed himself to be the son of God and the brother of Jesus Christ, sent to reform China.

The Chinese nation suffered a humiliating defeat when the Japanese destroyed the Chinese navy in the Sino-Japanese War of 1894–95. During the Boxer Rebellion of 1900, anti-missionary "Boxers" besieged the foreign legations in Beijing, prompting an eight-nation alliance to retaliate by storming, occupying, and looting Beijing. Educated men and women – many of whom were in exile – unleashed the Republican revolutionary movement, which overthrew the Qing dynasty in 1911 and led to the establishment of the Republic of China in 1912. It was just prior to this time that influential male intellectuals such as Liang Qichao called for the emancipation of women, better female education, and women's participation in nation-building as "conducive to the state's welfare and the goal of national survival," according to the volume *The Birth of Chinese Feminism: Essential Texts in Transnational Theory*, edited by Lydia H. Liu, Rebecca E. Karl and Dorothy Ko.

The Euro-American and Japanese invasions and colonial territorial concessions created pressures on China's economy that hurt women in particular, because female labor was critical to the household economy. "No mere 'supplement' or 'sideline' (as many economists and economic historians continue to call it) to a preexisting supposedly proper male-dominated economy, female-dominated spinning and weaving activity was a central and necessary element of the functioning of any rural household economy," write Liu, Karl and Ko. Women were forced to work more for fewer returns as the rural economy deteriorated, in part because of tariffs imposed by the British in favor of urban industries. As a result, women were increasingly "mortgaged to 'owners' – whether in the factory and brothel or in families to men who had bought them as servants, brides, or concubines – often for a lifetime," according to Liu, Karl and Ko.

In response to the exploitation of women at the end of the nineteenth century, anarcho-feminist He-Yin Zhen wrote a series of radical and visionary essays in 1907–08, which are analyzed and comprehensively translated into English for the first time in Liu, Karl and Ko's edited volume. He-Yin Zhen was long ignored in modern Chinese history. Scholars commonly referred to her as He Zhen, but she preferred to sign her family name as "He-Yin" in order to include her mother's maiden name. In 1907, He-Yin inaugurated the feminist journal *Natural Justice* (*Tianyi bao*), which she edited in Tokyo with her husband, Liu Shipei. The authors point out that the earliest Chinese translation of the first chapter of Marx's *The Communist Manifesto* was published in *Natural Justice*. Therefore, rather than the Communists bringing feminism to China, as is the narrative in official Party history, *feminism* first introduced Communist ideas to China through Japan, observe Liu, Karl and Ko.

He-Yin Zhen named barriers to women's property ownership as one of the primary ways in which men subjugated women. In her essay, "Economic Revolution and Women's Revolution," He-Yin decried the fact that in China, "when a father dies without sons, a relative's son is installed as the heir and inherits the wealth." In He-Yin's provocative essay "On the Revenge of Women," published in 1907, she called for the abolition of private property and the establishment of communally owned property in order to achieve economic equality between women and men. She launched a scathing attack on Confucianism (here translated in Liu, Karl and Ko's book):

Ancient teaching held that the wife is to the husband as the minister is to his lord, therefore men come first, women last; men are superior and women inferior. On the basis of "men first, women last," such other deviant teachings as 'yang initiates, yin harmonizes' or 'men act, women follow' were concocted to restrict women's freedom. And, from 'men superior, women inferior' such deviant teaching as 'the husband is the heaven of the wife' also came into being. The husband is thus made into heaven and the wife earth; the husband becomes identified with yang and the wife yin. *The relationship between men and women thus became one of absolute inequality* [through cosmic abstraction]. I cannot but sigh at this.

He-Yin Zhen's indictment of Confucian thought is one of the most comprehensive in Chinese history, rejecting Confucianism "as textual practice, as a system of ethics and thought, and also as a structure of sociopolitical and economic arrangement." Liu, Karl and Ko argue that He-Yin's writing was as prescient and historically important as "Elizabeth Cady Stanton's shocking feminist attack on biblical scholarship in America" in her 1895 book *The Woman's Bible*, or as "Simone de Beauvoir's dissection of the anti-woman biases of Western thought in mid-twentieth-century France" in *The Second Sex*. A hundred years before American feminist philosopher and critic Judith Butler wrote *Undoing Gender* (2004) to deconstruct the concept of sexual difference, He-Yin was calling for the elimination of the *nannü* (man/woman) category of gender distinction, which formed the basis of patriarchal power and hierarchy in imperial China and Confucian thought, according to the authors.

He-Yin Zhen writes in her 1907 essay, "On the Question of Women's Liberation" (here translated by Liu, Karl and Ko):

The social system in China has enslaved women and forced them into submission for many thousands of years. In ancient times, men acquired proprietary rights over women to prevent them from being claimed by other men. They created political and moral institutions, the first priority of which was to separate man from woman (*nannü*). For they considered the differentiation between man and woman (*nannü youbie*) to be one of the major principles in heaven and on earth. Men thus confined women to the inner chamber and would not allow them to step beyond its boundaries....

Chinese men refer to their wives as *neiren*, "person of the inner chamber," or *neizi*, "the inner one." The word *nei* is opposed to the word *wai*, or "outer." By keeping woman as his own property, a man cloisters his wife within the walls and deprives her of her basic freedom.

Once again, Chinese history is echoed in the resurgence of rigid gender norms in the China of today. As I describe in Chapter 1, the notion that men belong outside (in public) and women belong inside (at home) has undergone a comeback over the past decade. The 2010 survey of the status of women carried out by the NBS and the Women's Federation found that almost 62 percent of men and almost 55 percent of women believed in this traditional gender division, an increase of eight and four percentage points respectively compared with a decade earlier. These traditional ideas that women belong in the home – married and subservient to the husband, no matter how violent he is – also underlie the continuing prevalence of violence against women in the home, and the systemic difficulties facing women who attempt to escape an abusive marriage (explored in Chapter 5).

Perhaps the most famous feminist revolutionary of the late Qing dynasty era, and a contemporary of He-Yin Zhen, was the cross-dressing Qiu Jin. Qiu denounced footbinding, left her husband and children behind to study in Japan, and wrote about the urgent need for women's emancipation. In 1906, Qiu returned to China and published two issues of a newspaper, *China Women's News* (*Zhongguo nü bao*), before the authorities closed it. Qiu championed financial and political independence for women, and repeatedly declared that women and men were born with rights to equality and liberty. Historian Louise Edwards analyzes Qiu Jin's anti-Qing writings in *Gender, Politics and Democracy: Women's Suffrage in China*. Here is an excerpt from Qiu Jin's essay "A Respectful Announcement to My Sisters":

> While the men of China are entering a civilized new world, China's women still remain in the dark and gloom, mired in the lowest of all the levels of hell's prisons, not even contemplating raising ourselves one level. Feet bound so tiny, hair combed so shiny; tied, edged, and decorated with flowers and bouquets; trimmed and coiled in silks and satins; smeared with white powders and bright rouges. We spend our lives only knowing how to rely on men – for everything we wear and eat we rely on men.

Qiu Jin worked as a teacher at the Datong Girls' School in 1907 after the closure of her newspaper, but the school was a "thinly disguised front for anti-Qing activities," according to Edwards. The school trained students in military affairs as well as other subjects. Qiu Jin was duly implicated in treasonous activities, captured, and executed for advocating the overthrow of the Qing dynasty.

In the years before and after the Republican Revolution of the early twentieth century, many progressive intellectuals seized on and supported feminist ideals. In 1919, a young Mao Zedong wrote the first of a series of essays in Hunan newspapers about the death of "Miss Zhao," who had killed herself by slitting her throat rather than consent to an arranged marriage. Mao concluded that because women in China could not achieve genuine individuality in life, they were only able to assert their will through suicide, according to historian Rebecca Karl's *Mao Zedong in the Twentieth Century World*:

> As such, Miss Zhao's predicament was symbolic, Mao wrote, of the socially charged marriage question in general: should women (and men) submit to marriages arranged by parents, or should they be allowed to choose their partners freely? If the latter, society would need to accommodate women in public places, where they still did not appear in great numbers. In this sense, for Mao, any solution to the problem of marriage and of female free will would require a complete overhaul of social norms, from those regulating the family to those regulating citizenship and the state.

It was also in 1919, on May 4, that students in Beijing – many of whom were women – demonstrated against the Chinese government's weak stand against the Versailles Treaty, which would give territories in China that had been surrendered by Germany to Japan, rather than returning them to China. This sense that China was capitulating to foreign interests added to growing calls by activists in the "May Fourth Movement" to overturn outmoded Chinese traditions. "China's intellectual class began to question naturalized assumptions about China's place in the world, and about ideologies behind core relationships in China itself – between the individual and the family ... and importantly, between men and women," writes Edwards.

In pre-Communist 1927 China, Nationalist (Guomindang) lawmakers began drafting texts to replace the Qing dynasty legal code with more progressive laws which attempted to transform women's property rights. When the Republican Civil Code went into effect in 1931, it explicitly broke the link between property inheritance and patrilineal succession, giving women the same inheritance rights as men in principle: "In this, the lawmakers were heirs to the May Fourth critique of the patrilineal family and its emphasis on succession as the root of so many of society's ills, especially the devaluation of women and the prevalence of concubinage," writes Bernhardt. Yet even then, the new law clashed with social customs, and actual practice was very difficult to change, she notes.

While Nationalist lawmakers acted to codify gender equality, Communist revolutionaries around the same time (with whom the Nationalists were fighting a civil war) also tied the emancipation of women to the transformation of society. From the early years of the revolution, China's Communist Party actively recruited women, promising to liberate them from the binds of family and tradition. Historian Gail Hershatter writes in *The Gender of Memory* that "the Chinese Party-state moved rapidly and forcefully to rearrange rural social relations and the categories through which they were understood. One of those categories was gender…" The Communists defeated the Nationalists in 1949, and just one year after the founding of the People's Republic of China the new Communist government passed the Marriage Law of 1950, which marked a breakthrough in women's legal rights.

The 1950 Marriage Law abolished exploitative practices such as arranged marriage, the purchase of girl brides and the complicated rituals of betrothal gifts marking the transfer of the woman from her father's to her husband's home. It set a minimum marriage age, allowed women to divorce, gave the young generation the right to choose their own marriage partners without meddling from their relatives, and gave women new rights to inherit family property. Nevertheless, several years after the law was introduced, party officials backed away from efforts to enforce it after encountering resistance from many parents and parents-in-law. Rural families were afraid that the Marriage Law would lead to the loss of (previously male-controlled) property, and men feared that the free choice of partners might mean that only smart and rich men would be able to marry, observes Hershatter.

In the meantime, the Communist Party had begun to initiate land reform even before it formally took control of China in 1949. It included women in the allocation of roughly equal holdings of agricultural land across the country. Yet, although women were publicly recognized as having the right to own land, they were "at risk of losing land if they moved through marriage or remarriage and the land was held by the household head (usually male)," anthropologist Ellen Judd writes in her paper "No Change for Thirty Years: The Renewed Question of Women's Land Rights in Rural China."

The initial period of land reform ended in the early 1950s with rural collectivization, when Mao Zedong moved to get rid of private property and industry altogether. By 1955–56, most of the rural land formerly owned by the wealthy had been incorporated into collectives. Then in 1958, Mao unleashed the disastrous Great Leap Forward, announcing that China would surpass Britain and catch up with America in steel production. The government set up large-scale people's communes in the countryside and families were urged to melt down household implements in backyard steel furnaces to meet production targets. Local officials competed with each other to report extraordinary successes in production, and statistics were widely falsified. Senior leaders diverted millions of farmers from agriculture to work in factories, and increased the mandatory procurement of grain from the countryside.

It was during this time that the government wanted to mobilize all of its citizens – including women – to boost industrial production. Women's labor had traditionally been agricultural, so the phenomenon of the "Iron Woman" was born to draw more women into previously male-dominated work. Karl explains:

> In the fields, they [women] drove water buffalo teams and tractors for plowing, traditionally a man's job. In the factories, women moved in droves into management, which combined administrative and labor roles. Women competed with one another and with men for high productivity. Those women who gained distinction in these competitions became nationally known as "iron women." This was the fulfillment of Mao's desire for and commitment to female "liberation through labor."

Official rates of women's participation in agricultural production reached 60–70 percent in 1957, then 90 percent in 1958 at the onset of the Great Leap Forward, according to Hershatter in *Women in China's Long Twentieth Century*. The Communist Party frames the 1950s as the age of "women's liberation," and for many women previously bound to the home, unable to participate in public work, it was. Yet for other women laboring in the countryside, it was a time of tremendous suffering.

"Being liberated [by the Party] was not true liberation," says anthropologist Guo Yuhua, who conducted years of ethnographic research on women's memories of 1950s' agricultural collectivization in a northern Shaanxi village for her paper "Collectivization of the Soul." Women were not just objects of mobilization in China's gigantic social engineering experiment in the 1950s; their "liberation" was an important symbol of the success of the proletarian revolution in the Communist Party's rendering of history, according to Guo. Yet in official Communist Party history, "we cannot hear the voices of women," says Guo.

The women of Jicun Village, northern Shaanxi province, told Guo that they performed all the domestic chores, including weaving their own fabric to make clothes for the family; making shoes for the family; producing their own soy sauce and vinegar to cook all the family meals; taking care of elderly relatives; and looking after the children. Then, during rural collectivization in the 1950s, women were required not just to continue shouldering their heavy chores at home but also to go out into the fields to perform agricultural work alongside the men all day, even when they had just given birth. If there was an elderly person at home, he or she could tend the baby while the mother went out to work in the fields. If the woman had a young child who was not yet of school age, the child could take care of the baby. But if neither of these alternatives was available, mothers laboring in the fields every day had no way to breastfeed their babies, and their experience was particularly miserable, according to Guo:

> In the collectivist period, all able-bodied women were required to show up for work at the allotted time in the mornings… [Villagers told Guo] "If the baby had no one to care for it, then tie it to the *kang* [a brick bed]" – in order to keep the baby from falling off, "attach a wooden stake or an iron rod, use a belt to attach it there, and tie the end around the baby's waist. If you could return home in the middle of the day, then [you could] feed the baby some milk; if the fields were far away, then the baby would go hungry."

Guo describes women as weeping uncontrollably when recalling the agony of having to neglect their babies day after day: "After working the whole day in the fields, they would come home and see their baby bawling and famished, covered in feces and urine." This kind of anguish for a mother was every bit as painful as physical disease, according to Guo. The female villagers in Shaanxi province were almost never able to remember what year they were talking about, but they marked the time through their vivid memories of the difficulty of childcare, the pain of disease, and the feeling of hunger.

A woman's duty at home was to prepare meals for the entire household, so she had to make sure that her children and husband always ate first, leaving her with the least amount of food, according to Guo. As a result, Guo finds that Shaanxi women had a sharper recollection of food shortages and hunger than did men in the rural collectivization period up to 1954–55. By 1959, these food shortages became severe because of the Great Leap Forward policies. Although accounts vary of the exact extent of mass starvation, most scholars estimate that by the end of 1961 between 15 and 30 million, perhaps more, had died in the worst famine of the twentieth century. The famine largely affected rural farmers, and took an especially high toll on women, children and the elderly, according to Karl.

Marriage and the erosion of women's property rights in the post-Mao era

Several years after the death of Mao Zedong in 1976, Deng Xiaoping came to power and China launched dramatic economic reforms, dismantling rural communes in favor of what is commonly called the "household responsibility system." The state still ultimately controlled all land, but it subcontracted most rural land to individual families, who were initially given short-term leases. The contracts were extended to fifteen-year leases in the 1980s, and extended again to thirty-year leases in the late 1990s. Yet the evolving rural land contract system in the post-Mao era steadily eroded rural women's property rights, since their rights to land were tied to their (male-headed) household association.

In many parts of China, the original distribution of contract land by the state in the 1980s allotted sons much more land than daughters, according to studies such as "Why Women Own Less, and Why it Matters More in Rural China's Urban Transformation" by sociologist Sally Sargeson, and "Gender and Rural Reforms in China," by anthropologists Junjie Chen and Gale Summerfield. It is beyond the scope of this book to consider the complicated way in which rural women's land rights have been violated over the past several decades. In essence, women in rural China today own far less land and assets than men, according to studies such as "Gender Inequality and Poverty in Asset Ownership" by Li Xiaoyun et al.

Multiple studies have found that rural Chinese women routinely lose land and housing to male family members, particularly through the norm of wives following husbands to their homes after marriage, or "patrilocal residence." Married women left their own villages to join their husband's household, so they lost rights to land in their natal village communities, although initially the state's adjustments to household land allocation also gave women new land in their husband's village. Officially, the land was held by the village committee and contracted to rural households. But in practice land contracts were negotiated with a male household representative whose name was on the document. Women could only have access to land through their relationship to men as wife or daughter. Sargeson finds that today, when village committees approve new housing, each adult son may be allocated a house site but adult daughters – and only one at that – may be given a house site only if there are no able-bodied sons. It is extraordinarily difficult for women to challenge these practices.

Studies have shown that most rural land contracts in China only feature a man's name. For example, *not one* of 281 villagers interviewed by Xiaoyun Li's research team in Sichuan, Shaanxi,

Gansu, Ningxia, and Jiangxi province had a woman's name on their land contract. Professor Sargeson recounts a 2008 interview with a woman farmer in Yunnan province, who said that land contracts are automatically registered in a man's name:

> It's the women who marry in; we're considered to be outsiders. Men are recognized as locals, the members of village households. So the village leaders always write the man's name. Usually they don't even ask us, just put everything under his name.

A seventeen-province survey conducted by Landesa Rural Development Institute in 2011 found that only 17 percent of Chinese land contracts listed wives' names. Sally Sargeson and Yu Song's study of 414 land contracts in Zhejiang, Fujian, Hunan, and Yunnan provinces found that less than 20 percent included women's names – meaning that more than 80 percent of land contracts are *solely* in men's names.

The dynamics violating rural women's land rights in China are similar to the experiences of rural women in other regions such as South Asia, Latin America, and Africa. Among landless villagers in China, 28 percent of women have lost their land as a direct result of marriage, divorce, remarriage, or widowhood, according to the 2010 nationwide survey on the status of women carried out by the All-China Women's Federation and NBS. By contrast, the same survey shows that only 3.7 percent of men lose land for family reasons.

A large body of scholarship demonstrates that Chinese women's property rights have steadily eroded in the post-socialist, rural-to-urban transformation. Nearly half of China's population is still rural, but China is arguably urbanizing faster than any other nation in the world, with 60 percent of China's population likely to be urban by 2020, according to state media projections.

As China urbanizes, new mechanisms have emerged to disadvantage women disproportionately in the state's reclamation of rural land, moving people from the countryside to the cities. Sargeson finds that when rural land is expropriated for urban development, most of the compensation is paid to the male-dominated village committee. Sargeson documents multiple ways in which village committees exclude women from compensation, such as exclusively making payment to men on the basis of patrilineal birthright; only counting women as village members until they marry; excluding from compensation women married to non-local men; granting single women only half the compensation given to their brothers, in anticipation of the women "marrying out"; or giving women's share of the compensation to someone else, usually the male household head.

Moreover, the small number of women who appeal to governments for their legal share of land compensation tend to be ostracized by their community and rejected by the authorities, "who find it politically expedient to placate village men angered by the paltry compensation sums that the governments have paid for land taking," according to Sargeson. She finds that out of 343 village households relocated to valuable, urban homes in Zhejiang, Yunnan, Hunan, and Fujian provinces, only 71 had included women's names on the house titles. While married men tend to own homes as individuals, most women achieve property ownership – and only jointly – by virtue of their status as the wife of a propertied man. In consequence, Sargeson concludes that China's rapid urbanization perpetuates the gender wealth gap: "While former village men accumulate value-producing property in the new urban space, most women are incorporated into urban economies and societies as propertyless, feminised workers in, unpaid domestic caretakers of, and dependents on assets owned largely by men."

As China continues to dismantle remnants of the Communist planned system in its transition toward a market economy, many traditional marriage rituals banned during the Mao era have resurfaced. One such ritual is described by some scholars and media as the "bride price" or "bridewealth", practiced widely in rural areas, when the groom's family is expected to make a betrothal gift to the bride's family, especially if there is a surplus of men in the village. (By contrast, a dowry was traditionally given by parents to their daughter when she married.)

Anthropologist Yunxiang Yan writes that rural women have benefited greatly from a rising "bridewealth" in recent years. In *Private Life under Socialism*, Yan describes the "collapse of patriarchal power in the politics of family property." Yan focuses on the northern Chinese village of Xiajia, where he observed an "increase in youth autonomy, a decline of parental power, and a rise of young women as active agents in family politics." He describes the helplessness of parents trying to cope with increasing demands from their married children, as newlywed couples have fewer incentives to remain in the father's family: "The younger sons tend to follow the examples of their elder brothers in demanding more from their parents for their own marriages (the most obvious indicator of this is their demand for new houses, which have become a necessary part of the bridewealth in recent years) and then leaving the family as soon as possible."

There is no doubt that the older generation in China has come under tremendous financial and emotional strain due to the aging of the population, and new social expectations that parents should provide their son with a home in order to help him attract a bride. But Yan neglects to examine the fact that the most valuable marital assets tend to belong solely to the man. Betrothal gifts in the form of material goods or cash were traditionally given by the groom's parents to the bride's parents. Yan writes that in spite of the state's criticism of traditional marriage gifts and rituals, the amount of money given as "bridewealth" jumped exponentially from RMB 200 in 1950 to RMB 28,500 in 1999 (US$3,400 that year). Yan argues that "the new form of *ganzhe* [betrothal gift converted into cash] … has enabled the bride to take control over most of the marriage finances, and consequently she has become more 'greedy' and more active."

The narrative of women, and brides in particular, as "greedy" and overly "active" is often reflected in the tendency of the state media and people in society to succumb to gender stereotypes. The Chinese state media frequently report exorbitant sums of money demanded from a bride's family for granting the groom the right to marriage. The *China Daily* published a "map" of bride prices in June 2013, listing areas across China where grooms are expected to offer the bride at least tens of thousands of RMB plus a house to convince her to marry. These reports are often picked up by foreign news organizations as further evidence of women's increasing bargaining power in the marriage market due to the sex ratio imbalance.

Yet, rather than accepting state media reports at face value, one must look at who is sponsoring these widely circulated surveys, question their objectivity, and ask what might be their motivation in perpetuating stereotypes about "greedy" women who demand money and new houses. In the case of the 2013 *China Daily* "map" of exorbitant "bride prices," top real-estate developer Vanke and the real-estate sales arm of the popular website Sina.com, "Happy Living" (*Le Ju*) carried out the survey. Chinese real-estate developers clearly boost their profit margins by perpetuating the notion that a man must buy an expensive home to attract a bride, even in China's largest cities, where the betrothal gift practice is actually very rare. (See Chapter 3 for more on how real-estate developers work with the matchmaking industry in line with the government's goals of promoting marriage and demand for property.)

The overwhelming evidence from urban areas is that the national shortage of women in China has not, in fact, given urban women the upper hand in the marriage market. In villages, as Yan documents, parents may command a large betrothal gift for their daughter if there are many surplus men. But who ends up with the cash? It often continues to go to the bride's parents only, or, if it goes to the marital couple, it is generally shared by both the bride and groom. As for the supposed benefits accrued by rural women, some studies suggest that, on the contrary, the shortage of women may be correlated with increased trafficking of women or higher incidences of rape.

Sargeson's extensive research on the gender asset gap in China debunks the myth that rural women are profiting significantly from betrothal gifts. Her research on rural women's property rights examines the issue of betrothal gifts and concludes that any benefit to brides is negligible compared with the absence of women's property rights and women's low awareness of their rights as individuals within the marriage. As Sargeson writes in "Women's Property, Women's Agency in China's 'New Enclosure Movement': Evidence from Zhejiang":

> what rights do rural women hold in household property? Marital gifts such as jewellery remain the property of brides. Cash and

consumer goods become the joint property of the couple. Yet major assets such as land contracts, vehicles and housing are usually registered under the names of household heads: typically, men.

My own research finds that for urban women and men marrying in cities such as Beijing and Shanghai today, the largest expense by far is the purchase of a marital home, which tends to be registered solely in the man's name. Among the few examples of young urban residents whose rural parents expect a significant cash gift from the groom's family, the rituals of betrothal gifts and other marriage exchanges are extremely convoluted, not legally enforced in contracts, and do not necessarily mean that the bride benefits at all.

Let's return to the example of Ding Shen, the Shanghai IT consultant who was determined to buy her own home and enjoy the single life when I interviewed her in 2012. When I revisited her in Shanghai a year later, in 2013, she was 28 years old and engaged to be married. Although she has been working in Shanghai for several years, she and her parents have a rural *hukou*, or household registration. Recall that although her parents are relatively well-off, they declined to contribute any money to her savings for a down payment on a home, and gave money to their nephew instead so that he could buy a property. Meanwhile, as Ding's boyfriend is the son of poor farmers, his parents are unable to contribute money toward the purchase of a marital home. Ding originally wanted to buy a home in her own name to preserve her sense of independence, but now that she is getting married she plans to pool her savings with those of her boyfriend toward the goal of buying a marital home together in Shanghai within the next few years.

Ding and her boyfriend will themselves pay for a wedding dinner in Shanghai for twenty or thirty friends. Her boyfriend's parents will host a wedding banquet in his home village, and her parents will host one in theirs. Both sides expect guests to bring red packets (*hongbao*) of cash, which will offset the cost of the banquets. The big headache for Ding and her boyfriend is the *caili*, or betrothal gift from the groom's family (referred to as "bride price" in British media reports). Ding explains that her mother was extremely insulted when her younger sister married in 2010 without having arranged for a betrothal gift for her mother from the groom's family:

> When my little sister married, her *popo* [the groom's mother] promised to give her around RMB 30,000 for the *caili*. But in the end, she didn't give the money to my sister; she gave it to her son instead [the sister's husband]. So my mother was very unhappy... Now I have to find a way to take care of this [the betrothal gift] and keep everyone happy.

Ding's mother has already told her that she expects to receive a betrothal gift from the groom's parents when Ding gets married. Since Ding's boyfriend's family has very little money, Ding and her boyfriend have discussed at length how to appease both sets of parents. Ding will contribute her savings along with her boyfriend's money to give his parents around RMB 30,000 RMB (US$4,900), which they can use as the "betrothal gift" to Ding's mother. Ding and her boyfriend will tell his parents to present the money to Ding's mother a week or two before the wedding, when they plan to meet for the first time. Ding hopes that her mother will give the money to her as a wedding gift, in which case it would come full circle back to her and her boyfriend.

> Our parents are going back and forth, bargaining over this [through their children] and we both think it's really bad. We hope our plan will work and we don't want his parents to have to pay, or everybody's feelings will be hurt... I just have to arrange one

> meeting between our parents just before the wedding to take care of this [dispute over the gift], because if I introduce them to each other too early, there might be other problems, which would make it even more complicated.

Since Ding and her boyfriend can't afford to buy a home yet, they will look for a two-bedroom rented apartment in Shanghai to share with Ding's other younger sister, who is only 23 and can't afford to rent her own place. In the meantime, Ding has not told her boyfriend of her desire to register her name on the marital property deed if they buy a home together. I asked her why she hasn't yet mentioned the issue. She responded that it will likely be several more years before they can save enough money to make the down payment on a home, so there is no point in discussing the deed now.

This chapter has shown how women's property and marital rights in China have expanded at times and contracted at others. History demonstrates that there is no linear progression toward greater gender equality, and that past gains can all too easily be lost. But there is no question that throughout history, women who were able claim property in their own right in China also enjoyed greater individual freedom and economic independence – whether a thousand years ago during the Song dynasty or today. Then, as now, economic independence gave women much more power in other areas of their lives as well. And today economic power is especially critical for a woman if she is to stand a chance of escaping an abusive marriage.

Chapter 5 explores the link between women's weak property rights and the rampant problem of intimate partner violence in China. Studies show that between one-quarter and one-half of Chinese men surveyed have committed sexual or physical violence against their partners. Yet most women in China who are abused by their partners find it extraordinarily difficult to seek help because the legal and social system does not protect them.

FIVE

Wives caught in China's web of abuse

When Wang Mei's husband first hit her in their Shanghai home, she immediately acted to protect herself and her newborn baby by calling 110, China's emergency number. That call unleashed a torrent of retaliatory violence and harassment, not just from Wang's husband but from his extended family as well. Four years later, she has lost her home and custody of her only child, a son. Since China lacks a specific law on intimate partner violence, the court did not consider Wang's multiple police and medical records of her husband's violence to be sufficient evidence of any wrongdoing on his part.

Government figures from 2010 state that one-quarter of China's women have experienced intimate partner violence. Yet feminist activists say that figure is understated. Li Ying, a women's rights attorney and head of the Yuanzhong Gender Development Center in Beijing, says many women do not admit that they are victims of domestic violence. "Ask a woman if she has experienced domestic violence and she will say, 'Oh no, of course not!'" says Li. "Ask her if her husband has hit her and she will say, 'Yes.'" Even when Chinese women report intimate partner violence, the police are often unwilling to protect them, and may even incite retaliatory violence from family members who blame the woman for seeking help. Li acted as the attorney for the parents of Dong

Shanshan, a woman murdered in 2009 by her husband after she had called the police eight times to report domestic violence. Her husband was sentenced to just six and a half years in prison for "ill treatment" of a spouse.

"Don't expose family ugliness"

Relatives introduced Wang Mei to her husband in 2008; within months they were married. "I wasn't thinking clearly," she says. "People around me pressured me to marry. I was already 26 years old, [and did not want to] become a 'leftover' woman." Wang and her new husband bought an apartment in the same compound as her in-laws, since they wished to maintain a close relationship with their son. In 2009, Wang gave birth to a baby boy. Two months later, her husband struck her on the head and she called the police. The police took down the couple's personal details, but paid no attention to Wang's injuries and simply recorded the incident as "family conflict." The police told Wang and her husband that they were both at fault for not resolving their dispute peacefully, then left.

Wang did not tell anyone other than the police about the incident, but several days later her in-laws accused her of "exposing family ugliness" (*jiachou waiyang*). When Wang and her husband argued again, he hit her even harder, angry that she had reported their private affairs. Since the police paid no attention to her injuries last time, on this occasion she went to the hospital to have the injuries recorded in her medical records. She assumed her husband would think twice about attacking her now that she had a formal medical record of the violence. But the abuse escalated.

Wang says she was up against "a whole gang of people" in fighting the abuse. Her husband, his parents and other relatives scolded her for making the family look bad. Her husband's aunt said that, as head of the household, the man had a right to hit his wife. Wang says her husband also tried several times to force her to have sex after their baby was born, but she fought him off. "I had just given birth, I didn't want to have sex," she says, adding "the bit of affection I had for him has been ground down." Wang's husband apparently complained to his parents that his wife was shirking her conjugal duty. Her father-in-law warned her that she was "upsetting the balance of the natural world" by refusing to have sex with her husband. Her mother-in-law said it was no wonder that the son hit Wang, because he had nowhere to release his "natural" urges.

Wang did not want to trouble her own parents at first, she says, but "paper cannot cover up fire." Her parents were angered by the husband's abuse, yet urged her to think about her child before leaving her husband. Wang filed seven formal police and medical reports of domestic violence. She sought the help of her neighborhood committee, the most basic level of China's government, which advised her to adapt to the situation or risk losing custody of her child. No matter where she turned for help, Wang was thwarted – by the police, by her doctors, by her neighborhood committee and by Shanghai Women's Federation officials, who, Wang says, told her that divorce was a drastic solution, and that she should "just put up with it" and "try to change him."

In 2011, Wang made the wrenching decision to leave her toddler with her husband and move into her parents' tiny apartment in downtown Shanghai to escape the violence. Her husband refused to let her see her son, so she went to his workplace, a local government agency, to try to seek help from his boss. The couple began arguing and the husband hit Wang in plain view of his colleagues, who had to pull him off her. Her mother later received a call from an anonymous man, threatening to kill Wang if she ever appeared at her husband's office again. Wang called her husband's boss to report the death threat. "This is your own private affair," the boss told her. "It has nothing to do with us."

Like countless other Chinese women, Wang was trapped in what some scholars call a "web of abuse." China is certainly not the only country with an epidemic of domestic violence. For example, professor of social work Mieko Yoshihama wrote in her paper "Web in the Patriarchal Clan System" about the "spider web" of intimate partner violence, which is maintained by the common Japanese ideology of male superiority. In Japan, victims of violence are often blamed by family, friends, and colleagues, and isolated by a lack of assistance programs and police protection – all of which reinforces the sense of entrapment in a web. Yet Yoshihama found that, unlike in China, when Japanese women took the risk of exposing what was considered "private and shameful," they were able to free themselves from the abuse and isolation.

In China, the absence of the rule of law and the role of police as enforcers of social stability rather than protectors of victims mean that abused women often *fall into further danger and retribution* by the very act of reaching out for help from others. China still has no specific law to prevent or punish domestic violence (at the time of writing in 2013). Chinese women's NGOs have lobbied for many years for a targeted law which would include measures such as applying for a restraining order to keep abusers away from victims of violence, but the government has failed to act. So even if a woman has carefully documented abuse at the hands of her husband, it is extremely difficult for her to secure a protection order.

Female victims of intimate partner violence can theoretically file charges against their partner under the Criminal Law of the People's Republic of China. Women's rights attorneys Guo Jianmei and Li Ying point out that Article 234 of the Criminal Law states that intentional injury is a criminal offence, and that Article 260 prohibits abuse of family members. In addition, China's parliament, the National People's Congress, passed a Law of the People's Republic of China on the Protection of Rights and Interests of Women in 1992, amending it in 2005 to prohibit "family violence."

Yet attorneys Guo and Li, addressing "Women's Rights Protection in China" in *Elusive Equality*, write that existing laws do not adequately protect women abused by their partners:

> Considering that gender-insensitive judges might adopt [a] very strict accreditation standard in their trials, only *long-term* and *repeated* behaviours that lead to serious physical damage of victims had been regarded as domestic violence... The consequence is that cases of minor physical injury are dismissed and victims are denied the justice and assistance of a legal approach... In current judicial practice, even if domestic violence is accredited in the judgment of a divorce case, the compensation tends to be far from adequate for victims.

When I spoke with Wang Mei again, in October 2013, she had just lost her lawsuit against her abusive husband for custody of her child, now 5 years old. Her marital home was registered in both her name and that of her husband. Since she moved out of the home to escape her husband's violence, she has been living with her parents in their small apartment. The judge ruled that her husband could continue occupying the marital home, in exchange for paying her a settlement equal to a third of the value of the home. Her husband fought for custody of his only son, and won.

Even though Wang went to the trouble of obtaining medical and police records of the multiple times that she was beaten by her husband, the divorce court referred to the violence merely as "family conflict." Moreover, marital rape is not considered a crime in China, so the court also refused to consider the times when Wang's husband tried to force her to have sex with him against her will. "[My lawyer] raised the issue of violence, but it didn't help my case. My bruises were beneath the skin, with only some bleeding on the surface... so they weren't considered decisive evidence," says Wang. Rather, the court viewed Wang's documentation of her injuries as simply a record of the husband and wife "mutually fighting each other," and refused to assign blame to the husband:

> I am very unhappy... I took the legal route and spent the money, but it was all completely useless. Even though the court lets me see my child, it's no use. China's legal enforcement, well, you know what it's like. I can't take a court official with me to supervise every time I try to see my son. The court just gives me a piece of paper. Everything is still like it was before... His [the husband's] family doesn't let me see my child. If I try to see him, I get attacked.

Cases like Wang Mei's are all too common, according to Feng Yuan, a leading activist with the Anti-Domestic Violence Network NGO in Beijing. "Domestic violence is the most easily tolerated, least likely to be prosecuted form of violence against women," says Feng. Her group recently conducted an analysis of media coverage which found that within just two months between seventy and eighty women had been killed in cases of intimate partner violence.

In 2003, the Anti-Domestic Violence Network collaborated with others to write a complete draft of a law on intimate partner violence and proposed it to China's highest law-making body, the National People's Congress. In 2009, they revised some of the language in the draft legislation in an attempt to make it easier to pass, Feng explains:

> Every year, deputies to the National People's Congress propose adopting a national law on domestic violence. We have made specific suggestions on how the police should respond, how medical facilities should respond, how judges should rule on cases of domestic violence, how organizations should respond, how universities and high schools should raise awareness of domestic violence… We work with the [All-China] Women's Federation, but also with different kinds of women's groups – formal and informal – to influence decision-makers within the system who might be sympathetic.

Yet, at the time of writing, in November 2013, more than ten years of lobbying had still not resulted in a law. Consequently, in most cases judges find it extremely difficult to rule that intimate partner violence has taken place, according to Feng.

Intimate partner violence can take many forms. Physical violence is obvious, but sexual violence within marriage – forcing a wife to have sex when she doesn't want to – is widespread and is not illegal in China, according to a 2013 UN study on intimate partner violence in the Asia-Pacific. The UN Multi-Country Study on Men and Violence in Asia and the Pacific surveyed more than 10,000 men and 3,000 women between the ages of 18 and 49 from six countries – Bangladesh, Cambodia, China, Indonesia, Papua New Guinea, and Sri Lanka.

The UN study found that one-half of men in its China survey had used physical or sexual violence against an intimate partner.

It also found that 72 percent of men surveyed who had perpetrated rape in China did not experience any legal consequences. These shocking numbers were not exclusive to China, and were even worse in some of the other five Asian–Pacific countries surveyed. "Across all sites in the study, the most common motivation that men reported for rape perpetration was related to sexual entitlement – men's belief that they have the right to sex, regardless of consent," authors of the study concluded.

"The widely accepted norms about masculinity are a major driving force for the prevalence of domestic violence against women," Wang Xiangxian, a Tianjin Normal University sociologist involved in the research on gender-based violence, told the *China Daily*. The survey of 1,000 men and 1,100 women in a county in southern China found that women are at higher risk of rape from a partner than from a non–partner. Of the women who had been raped, three out of five were raped by a partner. Some 40 percent of the women who had been abused by their partners were so badly injured that they had to take leave from work or stay in bed, according to Wang. "It's pointless to talk about the abstract idea of gender equality if we don't eliminate the prejudice that is accepted by individuals, communities, and even the whole society," Wang told the newspaper.

There are many media accounts of men publicly beating women on busy streets in Chinese cities, while bystanders do nothing to help and police pretend not to see anything. The state perpetuates a vicious cycle of domestic violence by leaving abused women legally and physically defenseless. In China's most famous case of domestic violence in years, multimillionaire Li Yang, founder of the language instruction company "Crazy English," admitted on Chinese state television that he had beaten his American wife, Kim Lee. He said on a talk show that a Chinese man who occasionally hits his wife should be forgiven. "I still think that things that happen at home …, well, a family's shame should not be aired publicly," Li said, before the couple's divorce was finalized.

"The system is designed to make you give up"

Whereas I have used pseudonyms for most of the private individuals depicted and quoted in this book, American Kim Lee has agreed to go public about the violence in her marriage and her landmark divorce from Li Yang. The details in this section come from interviews I conducted with her in Beijing following her divorce in 2013.

Kim Lee met Li Yang on a trip to China in 1999, when he was lecturing about "Crazy English," a way of learning the language that involved overcoming inhibitions through shouting slogans such as "Conquer English to Make China Stronger!" He convinced her to move to China, where she developed the business with him, wrote its books, and gave birth to their first daughter before they married. While Li Yang travelled for much of the time, teaching "Crazy English," Lee stayed in Guangzhou with their daughter. Lee had no bank account of her own, and relied on cash that Li Yang would give her every month.

Shortly before they married in 2005, home prices in China began skyrocketing, and Li Yang became obsessed with buying property. "He started this shell game of us moving every few months because the price would go up; we would sell the house, then move to another one," said Lee. They moved nine times in ten years, and Li Yang bought dozens of properties in addition to the ones in which they lived. But – as with many women in

China – Lee did not insist on adding her name to any property deeds because she accepted his argument that the names did not matter since they were a team: "I didn't care about property … I loved him and I took his word for it."

People ask Lee why she didn't leave him the first time he hit her, but she says it wasn't that bad at first:

> The first time, it was just a shove, and we're both very passionate people. And from the very beginning, people pulled me aside, and said: "You don't understand, this is China. He works so hard. You have to be softer *wenrou yi dian*." And I said, that's true, he does work really hard, I work with him. But then it gets to be more than a shove. Then you've already accepted a shove, so then you accept a slap. Then you're seven months pregnant, and you're getting kicked in the stomach and trying to fight with a clothes rack to protect yourself.

Li Yang violently attacked Lee in 2006 when she was pregnant with their second child, but she did not tell anyone about it except for her sister-in-law, who said: "It's nothing. All men are like that."

By 2009, they had three daughters in Guangzhou, and Li Yang continued his love of looking at and buying real estate:

> One night, we had stopped, we were supposed to be on an outing to a night zoo, but he sees a real estate development, so we have to go look at it. And I was really impatient and I was complaining, frankly. I said, "This is crazy, I don't want to look at houses, I don't even own a house," and we'd been fighting about this. He said: "This has nothing to do with you."

In the meantime, Lee had learned enough Chinese to understand the conversations her husband had with his sister about buying property while they drove around:

> I would be in the back seat, his sister would be driving, Li Yang would be in the front seat, and they would talk about these things in front of me like I was a stone, talking about, "Oh, we can sell

this apartment, it's up by so much money, so many square meters, we can sell that one and buy two more here." I began to feel – I'm the wife, she's the sister, but I have no say-so in any of these real-estate transactions, except that I suffer and I have to keep moving my kids… I started realizing, I had never lived in a house with my own name, and maybe if I did, I would have said, I'm not moving this time. So I just put my foot down. I said, "I don't want to do this anymore."

From the moment Lee mentioned her dissatisfaction with the marriage, her husband started transferring marital property out of his name to someone else's name: to his sister, his uncle, other relatives and friends. Lee was so worried about running the "Crazy English" business and taking care of their three daughters that she didn't pay attention to who exactly was getting the properties. She did not give permission for her husband to transfer ownership, but that did not stop him:

I was so stupid in retrospect… I think a lot of women fall into this trap too. I think they're in love, like I was, and it's so easy when you're in love to just go along, it's such a hassle otherwise. He says, "we'll just put it in my mom's name, my dad's name, my sister's name," and women just say OK.

Lee had thought about an exit strategy for years, but she was afraid that if she left her husband she would lose custody of her daughters and would be "destitute." In August 2011, Lee had finally had enough of the violence, and posted photos of her bloody head and other injuries inflicted by her husband on Sina Weibo:

There are two fears: fear of leaving and fear of staying. And I think every [battered] woman reaches that point, where the fear of staying is greater than the fear of leaving. And in spite of all those romantic times in the past, the day my head hit the floor in front of my three-year-old is the day that my fear of staying was greater.

Lee's husband bashed her head on the floor repeatedly in front of their 3-year-old daughter, who yelled out, "What are you doing? Stop, Daddy!" The three-year-old jumped on her father and only then did he let go of Lee. "I grabbed my passport, grabbed my cash, grabbed [my daughter], and went," said Lee.

Still dazed from the beating, Lee managed to take her daughter with her to the police station to report the abuse, but they said they couldn't do anything without her husband present as well. He refused to go, sending a text message that he had only hit her ten times: "I was not that cruel," he wrote. The police gave her a slip to obtain a medical examination at a military hospital, but didn't tell her that she needed to pay almost RMB 2,000 (around US$320) in cash for the check-up. Lee normally only carried several hundred renminbi in her wallet, but by chance she happened to have a lot of money in her wallet that day because she was planning to pay the gas bill. She used RMB 1,800 to pay the hospital for a check-up, a CT scan of her head, and X-rays. Even though she felt humiliated, she took off her top and let male staffers take photos of injuries on her head, back, knees, and elbows, thinking that she could use the evidence to have her husband charged with attempted murder.

But when Lee consulted a lawyer, she was told that in order to have her injuries count as legal evidence of assault, she had to get a check-up at an "approved" crime hospital instead. "All those bills, I had Demerol for pain, whiplash, a concussion... I was livid. You mean this doesn't count?" Lee said. So a week later, she had another check-up at an "approved" hospital, but by that time her concussion had subsided and her injuries were not considered severe enough for Li Yang to be charged with attempted murder.

Fortunately, Lee had posted detailed photos of her injuries on Weibo. The pictures went viral and her followers jumped from a few dozen to tens of thousands. She realized that while the police and legal system had failed her, she could use her husband's fame as the "Crazy English" founder against him. "My Weibo pictures were my insurance policy, that my records wouldn't be swept away," she said. In September, Li Yang admitted in a Weibo post that he had beaten his wife. "I formally apologize to Kim… I committed domestic violence against her," he wrote.

As an American, Lee could have avoided the Chinese legal system altogether. "One side of me, the American, thought, I can be all the way on the other side of the world, away from all this. But on the other hand, I have three girls who are half-Chinese: is that the right thing to do?" she said. The moment she posted her first photo of her injuries on Weibo, she started receiving an outpouring of private messages from other Chinese women who had suffered horrific violence at the hands of their partners. Some wrote of broken bones, cigarette burns; some asked her to delete their message as soon as she had read it, because if their husbands found out, they would be beaten even more; many wrote that they couldn't leave their husbands because they would lose their home and custody of their child:

> So many women wrote to me about their failed divorce attempts.
> They would go to court and the husband would say, "She just
> fell off her bike," or "She bumped into a door." And the woman
> would say, but I have here the police report. But the police report
> just says "family conflict"; it doesn't say domestic violence or that
> he beat her. Even when women have evidence in court, the judge
> just dismisses it.

Lee said it was because of the helpless situation of so many other abused Chinese women that she decided to stay in China and fight her case through the Chinese system:

Every time I went on television, I wanted so much for someone else, a Chinese woman, to be with me, even if she didn't show her face, because I didn't want the message to just be that I am American. No one said to me, "Hey, you're American, we're going to wait on you in five minutes." I sat in the police station for six hours just like a Chinese woman. No one said, "Oh, because you're American, sit here in this comfy chair and we'll get the female photographer." No. I had the male photographer. I had to take my clothes off; I had a thin piece of cheesecloth in the crime hospital, like a Chinese woman would. The difference is, I had all those Chinese women's voices in my head, so instead of saying, "I can't do this" and running out, which I wanted to do, I just stood up. I took off my shirt, lifted up my arms, let them take the pictures. Without thousands of people pushing me on, I wouldn't have had the confidence to do it.

Lee became a heroine to tens of thousands of women across China; but she also faced a great deal of public hostility for trying to undermine a famous businessman, and trying to "split up everything that he owns." But Lee says that she wrote all the "Crazy English" textbooks herself and ran the business together with him:

It was my work and my writing of those books and my money that helped buy those houses, even if it wasn't out of my bank account. So that to me was something that I really felt angry about… *We* bought that property [together]… But even if I hadn't written those books, I was there. I was raising our kids. I was supporting him as a wife, and I did that in lieu of my own career, going out and writing books for myself, and putting money in my own bank account.

One day, when Lee was taking the subway with her youngest daughter, a man spat in her face and screamed: "I hope he beats you to death next time, you American bitch." That day, she called the US embassy, which recommended only that she leave the country. She took her daughters (who are US citizens) to

America to obtain emergency custody and keep them safe, then she returned to Beijing by herself, determined to fight Li Yang in court.

Throughout the court trials, Li Yang sent her explicitly violent text messages and pounded on her apartment door, threatening to kill her. One of the text messages said: "Sooner or later, you're going to be run down in cold blood in the street. A car could run you over, anything could happen. This is China." Another time, Li Yang told her in person: "I can hire someone to hit you, run you down with a car on the third ring road [a major highway in Beijing, near where Kim Lee lives]. I will be on stage in another city, and I will never be blamed, so you think about that." Each time Lee received a threat, she went to the police to report it, but they told her, "That's just words; that's not a crime in China." Lee explains:

> When the police said, "We don't do that, the court does that, you need to go to the court," I went to the court and I said "I want a protection order," … this is my life we're talking about. And the court said, "We need evidence, we don't have any evidence, the police have to have evidence, you need go to the police." I'd just been to the police, and I'd go right back to the police… It's like a ping-pong game and it fits into that overall theme: the whole system is designed to make you give up.

No Beijing court had ever issued a protection order before, and they did not give Lee one now. So Lee posted each threat on her Weibo account, and gave regular interviews to journalists to keep the spotlight on Li's violent behavior. She also hired a personal security guard and took her lawyer's advice to expedite the divorce case by not trying to claim any of the company profits. Rather, she focused on the real estate Li owned because it was tangible and at least some of it could be identified.

At the first trial, the judge asked Li to declare his income and assets. He said he made RMB 4,000 a month (about US$630) and owned nothing, not even a car or an apartment. This would have constituted perjury in a court in the United States, but the Beijing court did not consider his perjury to be a prosecutable offense. Kim Lee refuted his claim and gave the addresses of properties she knew were his, so the judge gave Li Yang fifteen days to prove that he didn't own the properties. Li openly defied the court and never gave any evidence of his wealth, despite the fact that he is widely known as a multimillionaire and successful businessman.

Since Li Yang denied that he owned any property, Lee then had to pay for an independent court investigation to assess the value of his properties. Lee knew that her husband had bought multiple homes around China, but she was most familiar with properties he had bought in Guangzhou, so she directed the investigators there. The court tried to delay the investigation for several months until after the Chinese New Year, but Lee kept the pressure on through her media interviews and Weibo posts, so finally a team was sent to Guangzhou, where they identified twenty-three properties in Li Yang's name.

Then, at the third court hearing, Li Yang's lawyer announced that the couple had only legally married in 2010, when they conducted a marriage ceremony in China, and insisted that their 2005 wedding in the United States did not count because the marriage was not legally binding in China. It turned out that Li had committed bigamy, and was still married to another woman in China when he married Lee in the United States. Li did not divorce his first wife until 2006 – a full year after he married Lee. Even though bigamy is a crime in China, the Beijing court said that it could not proceed with the division of properties in the divorce because Li was married to two women, and that his first wife must be brought back to Beijing so that she could share in the properties as well. After the third trial, Lee posted on her Weibo account: "Powerful and rich people can use bigamy as a way to postpone a divorce settlement."

Li Yang had helped his first wife emigrate to Canada. Lee told the judge that she would not give up her lawsuit; she would ask the Canadian embassy if he had committed immigration fraud. As soon as she mentioned this, the judge immediately ruled that the first wife no longer needed to appear in court, and the case was wrapped up swiftly.

Court investigators refused to consider as marital property all of the properties that Li had transferred to his sister and others, despite the fact that he did not obtain his wife's permission to do so. They also ruled out many other properties for one reason or other. The court finally settled on eleven homes that were still in Li Yang's name and had been purchased after his marriage to Lee, divided their value in half, arriving at the total sum of RMB 12 million (around US$1.9 million), which was barely enough to buy one three-bedroom apartment in downtown Beijing.

In February 2013, in a landmark ruling for China, the court announced that it was granting Kim Lee a divorce on the grounds of domestic violence, something that very rarely happens given the absence of a law on intimate partner violence, according to feminist activists. The court also issued the first ever restraining order in Beijing, which held for three months. Finally, it ordered Li Yang to pay a fine of RMB 50,000 for committing domestic violence – extremely rare in Beijing. However, women's rights attorney Guo Jianmei told Didi Kirsten Tatlow of the *New York Times* that, despite the symbolism of the legal ruling, the court had failed to uncover

Li Yang's true assets, and that the financial settlement of RMB 12 million was far too small, given his actual wealth:

> It's a huge flaw in the system. The state doesn't intervene to force rich men like Mr. Li to reveal their true assets, and it doesn't allow lawyers like us to do it either, it doesn't give us the rights. This is a society that doesn't control those with money or power. It doesn't see things through to the end.

Nonetheless, Lee says her legal battle is about much more than just receiving a divorce settlement from Li Yang. Women have stopped her on the street dozens of times to share their personal experiences of intimate partner violence and to thank her for speaking out on the issue:

> Last time, when I was on the [Beijing] subway line 1, a woman came up to me and rolled back the collar of her expensive blouse to show a yellow and purple bruise on her shoulder. One woman in the shopping mall lifted up her sleeve to show me the cigarette burns on her arm... Two women said they went to the hospital, and between the hospital and the police station their medical records were mislaid.

Lee's mission is to keep lobbying for a national law to tackle intimate partner violence:

> This is really an open sore. It's hidden, but it's hurting. When I put those pictures [of my injuries] on Weibo, I started a dialogue that needed to happen. Because domestic violence can't stop until there are better laws, and there aren't. The excuses are so flimsy: "Well, it's complicated" [say government officials]. They just won't pass a national law. And it's written. I have the draft. It's thorough, it's accurate and it's easy to enforce, but they won't pass it.

Many legal scholars have pointed out that, even if the Chinese government passes a new law specifically targeting intimate partner violence, there exists an enormous gap between Chinese laws on paper and how police and the courts actually operate. China fundamentally lacks the rule of law, and Chinese citizens are increasingly aware of the fact that the law does not adequately protect their rights. In his paper "Disappearing Justice: Public Opinion, Secret Arrest and Criminal Procedure Reform in China," legal scholar Joshua Rosenzweig writes:

> Public consciousness of individual rights and a desire for social justice have been building in China for more than a decade, and these attitudes have been reinforced and spread through awareness of individual miscarriages of justice revealed by a more active, professional media and shared through China's vibrant online communities.

As for Kim Lee, at the time of writing the Beijing court's protection order had expired, and Li Yang had paid less than a third of the settlement sum. The court has taken no action to force him to pay the remainder of the money; nor has it charged him with perjury or intention to pervert the course of justice. Meanwhile, Kim Lee has paid well over RMB 200,000 (around US$32,000) in legal fees as she attempts to enforce the court order, and she is also covering the costs of raising all three daughters by herself.

"Why should I give her a divorce? We're family"

Kim Lee was courageous and tenacious in her battle to expose China's epidemic of domestic violence. She leveraged her status as an American citizen who has rights in the United States to secure a major legal victory for battered women in China, who lack those rights. Yet the plight of most abused women in China is far worse than that of Kim Lee. For example, the Beijing municipal Women's Federation has set up women's shelters in the city, but *not a single woman* has used them, according to Xinhua News at the time of writing. Feminist activists say the shelters are unused in part because the government requires women to secure an official permit to stay there.

The lack of support for victims of intimate partner violence in China leads many to see themselves as failures, and such thoughts can lead to self-harm or suicide. Medical researchers Susan P.Y. Wong, Cuiling Wang, Mei Meng and Michael R. Phillips analyzed calls made by victims to a crisis hotline in China and wrote about their findings in a paper, "Understanding Self-Harm in Victims of Intimate Partner Violence." The researchers concluded that "turning to self-harm and death reflects the magnitude of the duress felt by victims who possess few resources and a narrow range of options to resolve the violence in their relationships."

Meanwhile, a 2009 survey of domestic violence against lesbians and bisexual women in China found that most was perpetrated by their *parents* or other relatives, rather than by their intimate partners, according to Tongyu, "Common Language," a Beijing rights group for lesbians, bisexual women and transgender people. The risks faced by the LGBTQ community in going public with family violence are obviously even greater than for heterosexual women (or men). "Coming out in China is not just an individual statement, it is a political act," says Xu Bin, the head of Tongyu. Xu says that many LGBTQ individuals hide their sexual orientation in order to protect their parents, who might be ostracized or subjected to homophobic abuse. (See Chapter 6 for more on LGBTQ activism.)

Compounding problems for victims of intimate partner violence, it is extremely difficult to obtain a divorce if their partner is unwilling to separate, and especially so for women who are financially dependent on their partner. Legal scholar Margaret Woo writes in her paper "Shaping Citizenship: Chinese Family Law and Women" that "even if a female litigant procures legal assistance, she must meet a stringent, often impossible, burden of proof before the courts will act on a hidden asset claim." The often insurmountable legal barriers facing women seeking divorce from an unwilling partner effectively force many to remain in an unhappy, potentially violent marriage. Recall that according to the Communist Party, marriage and family form "the basic cell of society"; a "harmonious marriage" is the foundation of a "harmonious society" – code for social stability. The Chinese state wishes to preserve as much as possible the outward form of marriage, but whatever violence takes place within that marriage is considered purely a private matter, categorized by the courts as "family conflict."

Consider the case of Han Zhao, a 45-year-old accountant in Shanghai, whom I interviewed in 2012. I chose him as an interview subject when searching for married couples with property registered in both names, as opposed to just the man's name. I hoped he could shed light on how egalitarian relationships work in China. However, during the interview Han's description of the way he treated his wife sounded manipulative at the very least. He did not introduce me to his wife, so I could not independently verify what he said. His perspective sheds light on how difficult it is for women to leave a bad marriage.

Han had bought a large house in Shanghai's Pudong district when it was just developing in 1997. At the time, the government was beginning to privatize urban housing, so it had a policy of offering incentives for residents from other parts of China to buy homes on the Shanghai market. Han originally had a Beijing *hukou* or household registration, but by purchasing a 200-square-meter home he was able to secure two Shanghai *hukou* permits, one for himself and one for his wife, a Beijinger whom he married in 1998. An indication of how high property prices have climbed since the late 1990s is that he only had to pay a total of RMB 600,000 (around US$72,000 in 1997) for the home. Before they married, Han's wife had what he called a "successful" career in human resources management in Beijing. But he convinced her to give up her job and move to Shanghai with him to start a family. That year, they also purchased a much smaller marital apartment, which they registered in both names.

Soon after they had married, Han's wife gave birth to a son. They began fighting frequently at this time; after the fights, his wife often took her son to her parents' house in Wuhan, Hubei province, said Han. He complained that his in-laws always took her side and not his: "In China, marriage isn't just between two people; it's between two families." In spite of the fighting, in 2004 the couple had another child in Wuhan, a daughter, for whom they had to pay a family-planning fine of several thousand renminbi because they had broken the city's one-child policy (although the fine was much smaller in Wuhan than in Shanghai).

Han hadn't had a regular job for years, saying only that he lived off "investments" in real estate. In 2005, some of his investments went bad, so he sold the marital home, which was jointly registered. And in 2007, he also had to sell the large property in Pudong, which was registered solely in his name. Han did not say if he ever hit his wife, but in 2010 she told him she wanted a divorce, and took both their children back with her to her parents' home in Wuhan. He then said he used their children to "tie up" (*shuan*) his wife: "I went to Wuhan and secretly took the kids back to Shanghai with me, so she had no choice but to return here," he said. When his wife came back to Shanghai, she filed a divorce suit against Han: "I don't understand why she was making such a scene. We were living together just like normal people, but she still insisted on filing for divorce – really unbelievable!"

The couple had a mediation (*tiaojie*) hearing before a judge. Han presented his case for why his wife shouldn't get a divorce, and his wife presented her case for why she wanted to leave the marriage. The judge sided with Han and urged the wife to stay with her husband. As Han put it:

> This judge was very reasonable… He advised her: "You have two kids, you don't have a job; if you divorce your husband, who are you going to depend on for a living? Your *hukou* is here in Shanghai, so you can't return to Wuhan." So the judge didn't allow it… and my wife just gave up. The economy is bad, so we'll just keep getting by.

Han's wife decided not to pursue the divorce case any further and found work as a cashier at a grocery store, making around RMB 2,000 a month (US$310 in 2012), which Han says is "just enough to buy food for the family." She is responsible for buying food and cooking all the meals, while Han pays for utilities from unspecified "investments," as he still does not have a job. Since he sold their homes, they are now living in a house owned by his mother. "I try to avoid seeing my wife, so I come home very late at night," said Han. I asked him why he doesn't want to agree to a divorce, since he dislikes spending time with his wife anyway. "Why should I give her a divorce? We're family," he said.

This chapter has focused on China's hidden epidemic of intimate partner violence, which is the worst possible outcome for a woman who rushes into marriage with the wrong partner out of fear of becoming "left over." Let us briefly look again at the web that ensnares many young women in urban China.

When an educated, urban woman enters her mid-twenties, she comes under intense pressure to marry before she becomes "left over" and, according to the state media, very few men would want her. The anxiety a young woman feels about possibly never being able to find another husband places tremendous pressure on her to make excessive compromises in choosing a marriage partner. The state media, parents, friends and colleagues send a barrage of messages telling her that she should stop focusing so much on her career and spend her time finding a husband instead. The young woman may well have experienced gender discrimination in hiring and promotion, but even if she has been successful in her career in spite of entrenched sexism, she may begin to turn down promotions in her late twenties out of fear that potential suitors will find her too intimidating and unsuitable for marriage.

If the woman does find a good fiancé, the strong social norm of male home ownership and home buying upon marriage places intense pressure on her to leave her name off the marital property deed. In many cases, the woman will use her life savings to help purchase a marital home, which is likely to be registered solely in the man's name. The young woman probably wants an equal relationship in the marriage and wants to put her name on the property deed. She may even fight with her fiancé to register her name on the deed along with his. But, in the end, she is likely to succumb to the pressure to marry out of fear of not finding another husband, so will probably not walk out on an unequal financial arrangement. According to the 2011 interpretation of China's Marriage Law, if the woman does not have her name on the property deed, she will probably forfeit her claim to the marital home, unless she goes to extraordinary lengths to document her financial contributions.

Even if the woman earns a very high income, the fact that the most valuable asset in the marriage, real estate, is registered in her husband's name is likely to reduce her bargaining power in the relationship. Since the typical woman possesses far less wealth in the marriage, has weak property rights, and is not permitted to share a bank account with her husband (at the time of writing), she is more likely to remain trapped in the marriage if her husband is abusive.

If an abused woman tries to seek help from the police, from the courts and from family, she is unlikely to find the support she needs to escape a violent marriage. By seeking help openly, she may open herself up to further retaliatory violence from extended family members for "exposing family ugliness" to outsiders. A court is extremely unlikely to rule in favor of an abused woman, because there is no specific law preventing intimate partner violence and marital rape is not a crime in China, so the perpetrator of the violence is likely to suffer no legal consequences for his actions. Even if the woman manages to sue her abusive husband successfully in court and the court rules in her favor, the ruling is often not enforced, according to feminist activists.

Given the lack of legal protections for women who are abused in marriage, or whose property rights are violated, what can women do to protect themselves? Chapter 6 explores the ways in which Chinese women resist systemic gender discrimination, in spite of the repressive state security apparatus.

SIX

Fighting back

Women's resistance in the authoritarian state

Li Maizi is the public name of a 24-year-old feminist activist who grew up in the countryside outside Beijing. Openly lesbian, university-educated, an only child of poor farmers, Li lives with her girlfriend in a rented apartment in Beijing. She is one of several low-paid employees of an unregistered grassroots women's rights group which has organized public acts of "performance art" to protest gender discrimination.

"In China, the space for activism is very small, so if it's a direct and public action, then we cloak it with the outward appearance of art. So the outward form is gentle, but the content is powerful," says Li, who does not wish to disclose the name of her group for fear of being shut down by the government.

Since the founding of the People's Republic of China in 1949, various forms of authoritarianism have prevented the formation of a spontaneous, large-scale women's rights movement. Feng Yuan of the Anti-Domestic Violence Network in Beijing says there is a difference between the Communist Party's "movement of women" (*yundong funü*) – a top-down mobilization of women in service to the nation – and a bottom-up "women's movement" (*funü yundong*). "Outside of the government's official mobilization of women, there is basically no space for an independent women's movement," says Feng. Feng's own group is a "non-governmental organization," but is registered with the government and required to work in alignment with agencies such as the All-China Women's Federation. (See Chapter 5 for more on the role of NGOs in lobbying for legislation to tackle intimate partner violence.)

Some of China's most radical feminists, like Li Maizi, do not belong to any officially registered organization, choosing instead to work outside the system to bring about a greater awareness of women's rights in Chinese society. For example, in 2012 Li and other young women dressed in white wedding gowns splattered with red, blood-like paint in downtown Beijing to highlight China's epidemic of domestic violence. They posed for photographs holding placards that said, "Violence is right beside you. Why are you still silent?" and "Love is not an excuse for violence." Li and other volunteers also distributed postcards of their naked torsos, some splashed with red paint, in a campaign to collect 10,000 signatures to push for legislation on intimate partner violence.

In the "Bald Sisters" campaign, Li and three other young women shaved their heads in public in the southern city of Guangzhou to protest gender-based quotas favoring men in university admissions. Many university programs require women to score higher than men in entrance examinations, apparently in response to the fact that women now outnumber men at both undergraduate and Master's levels, according to the Ministry of Education. Li and other volunteers shaved their heads in support of a female student who was rejected from the University of International Relations after scoring 614 on her university entrance exam, or *gaokao*, which was below the required score for female applicants of 628. Were she a man, she would have been admitted: the program requires male applicants to score only 609.

After the Guangzhou campaign was covered in the Chinese media, women also shaved their heads in Beijing, Tianjin, Shanghai, and other cities to protest widespread gender discrimination in university admissions. Lü Pin and Huang Yizhi from the Media Monitor for Women Network NGO followed up by writing a formal letter to China's Ministry of Education, complaining of discriminatory policies against women, which the Ministry said were necessary "to protect the national interest."

Li Maizi does not use the word "protest," preferring to speak of "actions" (*xingdong*). "Our actions are not very politically sensitive compared with other, more extreme actions, because we want to cooperate with the traditional media, so we choose topics that are more mainstream," she says. Since Li's group receives very little funding, members write their own news reports on their gender "actions," hoping the message will get out. Li says that of all the feminist "actions" she has helped organize, the "Occupy Men's Toilets" campaign had the greatest impact.

In February 2012, several female volunteers in Guangzhou occupied some men's toilets and invited women into the vacated men's stalls to shorten their typically long wait. The volunteers held up placards saying, "More convenience for women, more gender equality" and called on local governments to provide more public toilets for women. The protest received widespread media coverage, in response to which Guangzhou officials later pledged to increase the ratio of women's toilets to men's. "This issue isn't that politically serious, but it's a problem every woman has to deal with every day, so many women and men were able to see the inequality and to support the cause," says Li.

Yet when Li's group organized the same campaign in the Chinese capital, Beijing, it found that the environment for public actions or gatherings of any kind was more repressive than in southern China. Several days after the Guangzhou protest, Li and several volunteers tried to occupy some men's public toilets in downtown Beijing, but a group of police officers told her that they were assembling in public without permission. They detained her and another volunteer at a nearby restaurant for the rest of the day.

"The police came and asked who the organizer of the action was, and I said, 'I am,' which was very stupid," says Li. "I really should have just run away, but I didn't have enough experience then." That night and for some time afterwards, the keywords "Occupy men's toilets" were blocked on Sina Weibo, and the police began to monitor Li's phone calls. Li had planned another action against the requirement that all women applying for civil service jobs undergo an invasive gynecological examination to screen for sexually transmitted diseases and malignant tumors. She was intending to hold a placard in front of the civil servants' personnel office, calling on government departments to drop the requirement, but the police showed up on her doorstep the morning of the action and took her to the police station "to drink tea" – a euphemism for interrogation.

"What are you planning to do?" asked the police. Li did not divulge any details and spoke instead about other matters.

"Are you planning a protest in front of the civil servants' office?" asked the police.

"Oh, so you know everything already," replied Li.

"You are not permitted to do it! You are also not allowed to write about this on Weibo! You are not allowed to do anything!

Just go home and wait there quietly until you get further instructions from us," said the police.

Li went home. The following morning the police knocked on her door again at 7 a.m., fearing that she would proceed with her protest, and took her back to the station. They also dispatched officers to monitor the entrance to the civil servants' personnel office in case other activists appeared. At the time, Li was a senior in college, so the police called her university to complain that she was a troublemaker who needed to be controlled. The university vice president summoned Li for a talk in his office, and offered her a work-study position on campus for RMB 120 a month in exchange for her staying out of trouble. Li laughed at the gesture and told the vice president: "How's this instead? I'll give you RMB 250 and you give me back my freedom." The university prohibited her from taking part in activities off-campus, but she sneaked out several times anyway before her graduation that summer.

The difficulty Li Maizi experienced in organizing a simple call for more public toilets for women illustrates the elaborate "stability maintenance" (*weiwen*) system set up by the Chinese state to absorb popular protests and ensure the ruling Communist Party maintains its grip on power. Sociologists Ching Kwan Lee and Yonghong Zhang detail in their 2013 paper "The Power of Instability: Unraveling the Microfoundations of Bargained Authoritarianism in China" how the state is able to manage social unrest, manifested in the dramatic increase in "mass incidents" from 10,000 a year in 1993 (according to China's Ministry of Public Security) to 180,000 a year in 2010 (according to sociologist Sun Liping).

Through years of ethnographic research among grassroots Chinese officials responsible for "stability maintenance" in Shenzhen and Beijing, Lee and Zhang provide extraordinary insight into how deeply the "grassroots state" penetrates into local communities to gather information on citizens and defuse conflict that might threaten social stability. They write that one of the most common government strategies is to "buy stability" by making cash payments or giving other benefits to key people who stage public protests, or by drawing on local "stability maintenance funds" to pay for urgent services such as electricity or water supply when these become the target of protests. All district governments in Beijing, for example, had "stability maintenance" annual budgets in 2008, ranging from 1 billion RMB (around US$146 million in 2008) to RMB 2 million (US$295,000), according to their research. By bargaining with and fragmenting protesters, co-opting some and threatening others, grassroots Chinese officials absorb acts of resistance and achieve "authoritarian domination," according to Lee and Zhang.

Human rights activist and feminist writer/film-maker Zeng Jinyan has experienced the worst of China's "stability maintenance" apparatus. Zeng began blogging in 2006 about police persecution of her husband, Hu Jia, a leading critic of Chinese government abuses. Hu, winner of the European Parliament's Sakharov Prize for Freedom of Thought in 2008, has become such a famous dissident that many people only know Zeng Jinyan as his wife. When I met 30-year-old Zeng in September 2013, she indicated that most foreign reporters who have interviewed her over the years have only been interested in what her husband is doing or feeling. Although Zeng is well known for her marriage to dissident Hu, Zeng reflected that "we haven't had any time to manage a marriage, basically." For most of their marriage, Hu has either been in prison or in "forced disappearance," meaning that Chinese police have detained him without telling Zeng or anyone else where he is. In 2006, Zeng wanted to study abroad but she and her husband were both placed under house arrest, under strict police surveillance. Authorities also confiscated Zeng's passport in 2007 so that she could not leave the country.

Hu's constant disappearances and imprisonment meant that Zeng took sole responsibility for meeting the emotional, financial, and physical needs of their daughter and Hu's parents, all while being harassed by the police and prevented from holding a regular job. Zeng explains:

> When Hu Jia returned from his forced disappearance, we were still under house arrest. We had no psychological support, no financial support, no resources, nothing, except that some friends maybe would send greetings and make phone calls at first... So at that time I developed a concern for family members of political prisoners or rights activists. I eventually lost my job and the police harassed all of our relatives. I researched other families of rights activists and found out that many of them also lost their jobs or couldn't get any opportunities for future development... Usually, when a rights activist is detained, the parents' medical needs and children's educational needs can't be satisfied. So usually the wife is the only person to handle all of these problems.

Just forty-five days after Zeng gave birth to a baby girl in late 2007, police barged into their home in Beijing and formally arrested Hu Jia for "harming state security," a vague charge thrown at individuals seen as a threat to the government. A policeman asked Zeng to cooperate with them and provide evidence against her husband, but she refused. One policeman attempted to convince Zeng to leave her husband. "You have admirers elsewhere, try to get rid of your husband," he said. When that strategy failed, another policeman threatened to take Zeng's newborn baby away from her and allow her to breastfeed just once every few hours.

The police never followed through on this last threat, but during some lengthy periods of house arrest they refused to let Zeng take her baby outside. "My daughter needs fresh air and sunshine," Zeng pleaded with the police. "You can get that through the window," the police replied. During the times that Hu was at home, Zeng says, it was impossible to have a normal marriage while being forced to live with the police presence for weeks or months. "You want to keep your dignity. The police have a group of psychological experts and brainwashing experts, so you need to be very careful, and you're extremely nervous, and you overreact to normal things," she says.

Since 2006, Zeng Jinyan has gained worldwide recognition for her blog about the constant police surveillance (although authorities block access to the blog in mainland China). In 2007, *Time* named her one of "the 100 men and women whose power, talent or moral example is transforming the world." She and Hu made a video documentary, *Prisoners in Freedom City*, which vividly portrayed their experience of house arrest.

Yet Zeng was intensely lonely; her blogging was no substitute for real human interaction. "When Hu Jia was in prison or forced disappearance, many times I wished I was the person in prison because there are too many things out of prison you have to handle," she says. "I had been isolated by the police from society. Even though I could express myself a little bit on the Internet, I was personally isolated in real life."

Zeng used to consider herself a "very emotionally sensitive" person, but the years of extensive police interference in her daily life – especially since she became a mother – changed her:

I had to learn how to negotiate with the guards around me, around the clock. One time, on the June 4th anniversary [of the government's brutal crackdown on 1989 democracy protests in Tiananmen Square], I thought I would be put under strict surveillance, but I didn't know I was not allowed to go out to buy food. I wasn't allowed to go out and I didn't have anything in my fridge. I panicked... I need to suppress my emotions and my desire for anything, because if you don't have any needs, there won't be any opportunity for the police to pressure you. But it's impossible, right? As long as you have a child, you have needs. And you have to eat or you're going to die. You have to work to earn money... And your child needs to go outside every day.

For many years, Zeng could not sleep well because the police kept moving around in the middle of the night:

The police had to sleep on chairs on my staircase, so they had to move their chairs often to make themselves comfortable. I can understand. But it happened in the middle of the night very often, so it was also a kind of threatening message. That was at first. Later, I just dreamed about the police noises, whether they were there or not.

Zeng used to like her Beijing apartment because she felt it was a safe space for her to escape from the police harassment. Then one of the policemen warned her to be careful because when she was not at home the police would enter the apartment to check on things, so she no longer dared speak openly in her own home:

I knew my home was monitored, so I didn't talk too much. But there will be problems if you don't communicate with people around you. You have family problems and many, many other problems because it's difficult to speak out about what you are thinking... At first I thought, if I leak my emotions and feelings, it's very easy for the police to detect and it's risky... But if you continue to repress your emotions over a long time and you have no support, no communication; it's very difficult to handle the situation. The pressure is extremely intense, and in the end you'll just collapse.

Zeng says that a common method used by Chinese police to control rights activists is to pressure the wife or other family members, telling them to persuade the activist to stop making trouble. Relatives may lose their jobs as a result of the activism of someone in their family. Police have frequently harassed Zeng's parents, parents-in-law, and other relatives. "When my grandpa passed away, we went to his funeral and the police followed us every step of the way. The whole family clan was unhappy with me, Hu Jia and the police," says Zeng.

In January 2012, when Zeng was traveling for a project, she left her daughter alone with Hu for a few days in Beijing. Eight policemen entered their apartment, confiscated the couple's laptops, and shut their 4-year-old daughter in a small room for more than an hour while they interrogated Hu in the dining room. Following that incident, Zeng announced on Twitter that she was separating from her husband. After the US government mediated departure of the blind legal activist Chen Guangcheng from China in mid-2012, Zeng was able to obtain permission to move with her daughter and pursue graduate studies in gender and sexuality at the University of Hong Kong.

Even though Zeng is separated from her husband, she wants Hu to be an engaged parent, so she asked him to take care of their daughter for a few days in July 2013, while she spoke at a "BlogHer" conference for women bloggers in Chicago. But when Hu celebrated his fortieth birthday with their daughter and some friends at a restaurant in the southern city of Shenzhen, police again broke up the party and detained Hu. Zeng heard about his detention through Twitter, and she was seized with fear. She did not know where her five-year-old daughter was for several hours, until another friend told her that she was safe:

I was very nervous, so when I came back, I wrote my final will to arrange my daughter's life just in case I have an accident. I don't want my daughter to live with her father, not in everyday life. For some holidays it's OK, because maybe the risk can be controlled, but I don't believe it's OK over the long term... I need to have a back-up plan. So it's very sad actually, for him, for our daughter, and for me. Because anything could happen, even when Hu Jia is just having a birthday party... I wish that my daughter didn't have to understand these kinds of things at her young age. The later, the better. I just want her to have a normal, simple kid's life.

As a feminist blogger and gender researcher, Zeng knows all too well how the authoritarian repression of the state has dampened prospects for a nationwide women's rights movement in China. "Control is tightening on the whole of civil society, so I don't think there's any possibility of a real women's movement in mainland China," she says. Zeng also faults the international media for largely leaving women out of their stories on rights activism in China. For example, Zeng has studied the 2005 media coverage of hundreds of villagers – mostly women – who organized protests demanding the removal of the Taishi Village chief in Guangdong province for abusing his power. Prominent women's studies scholar Ai Xiaoming made a documentary about violent clashes with riot police at Taishi village, and she herself was beaten by police while filming. Yet Zeng says that the struggles of the female activists did not get enough attention in mainstream media. She cites a paper by sociologist Sophia Woodman, "Law, Translation and Voice: the Transformation of a Struggle for Social Justice in a Chinese Village," which argues that the village women largely "became a mere backdrop to the dramatics of mostly male 'heroes'." As Zeng explains, "I don't mean that the work of men is not important, but the process is that local women protesters' voices are carried by male heroes, most of whom are outsiders, so the original images and voices of women are obscured."

The voices of women are obscured in many contemporary depictions of China, not just in media reports about rights activism. Zeng Jinyan's experience as a persecuted dissident and single mother is obviously not representative of all women. Yet in some ways her heavy domestic burdens are common to wives and mothers throughout China, who work hard to support the household but whose contributions are invisible and unrecognized.

Another beleaguered rights activist and single mother is Ye Haiyan, also known by her blogger name "Hooligan Sparrow." In 2003, she stayed at the home of some sex workers, and was so moved by their experience that she started a website to help young women working in the sex industry. Her website was constantly hacked, and she began to think about quitting the campaign, but then she learned of the murder of a 23-year-old sex worker named Yaoyao, who had actively contributed to her site. Ye told journalist Paul Mooney:

> I was tired and people were opposing me and attacking me every day… But the death of Yaoyao gave me the determination to carry on. I felt their vulnerability for the first time. I began to understand their lives even better, and it was frightening.

In 2006, Ye Haiyan founded a grassroots women's rights center in Wuhan, but it was unable to register as an NGO. In the meantime, Ye took part in more visible protests calling for an end to discrimination against sex workers, who are reluctant to report violence by police or customers for fear of being arrested. For a time, Ye even had sex with customers for free in order to understand better the lives of sex workers. Ye was often harassed and "invited to tea" by the Wuhan police, and in 2011 she was forced out of the city back to her home province of Guangxi, where she continued to be harassed. In 2012, a group of men ransacked her small office.

Refusing to be cowed, in May 2013 Ye travelled to Hainan province to protest against child abuse in Chinese schools; a school principal there had been accused of raping six schoolgirls in a hotel room. Ye posted a picture of herself online holding a sign that said "Principal, get a room with me – leave the school kids alone." The post went viral on Weibo and thousands of Internet users across China – some of whom posed naked, some of whom were celebrities like artist Ai Weiwei – imitated her action by posting online pictures of themselves holding the same sign, or playing on Ye's original language.

Beijing women's rights activist Li Maizi was among many who shed their clothing to post an online picture in support of Ye Haiyan's protest. Yet what started out as an imaginative and popular Internet meme soon became yet another case of the state persecuting someone perceived to pose a threat to social stability: when Ye returned to her home in Guangxi province, several people charged into her home and attacked her. Ye tweeted on Weibo and Twitter that she was picking up a knife to protect herself and her young daughter, then fell silent. Police detained her for a couple of weeks and then charged her with wounding three women in a struggle. Following Ye's release from detention, she was evicted from several rented apartments, where the landlords had apparently been told not to allow her to live there. In another sign of the importance of home ownership to a Chinese citizen's security and well-being, Ye's supporters organized a fundraising drive in mid-2013 for her to buy a home of her own, so she would no longer be subject to eviction by landlords.

Activist Li Maizi observed: "Ye Haiyan was held by the police not because of her action against child abuse, but because she had already become known as a [politically] 'sensitive person'." I asked if Li and her girlfriend – also a feminist activist – ever feared being kicked out by their landlord because of Li's occasional trouble with the police. "We told our landlord we are women's rights activists and she supports us. She has two big dogs; the Public Security Bureau told her it's against the law to own big dogs in downtown Beijing. I said I could start an action to help her, and she said, 'yes, yes, yes!'" said Li.

Gender and LGBTQ activism

Only 24 years old, Li Maizi has been out as lesbian, or *lala*, for years. In university she founded a support group for lesbians because she discovered that China's rising gender inequality was not just confined to heterosexuals: it is also evident in the LGBTQ community. "Male gays are in the MSM (men who have sex with men) community, so they get a lot of funding for HIV issues, plus the media reports mostly on gay men and hardly ever reports on lesbians," says Li. "Chinese men are much richer than women, so many gay men have a lot of money too, and their sex life is considered much more lively. So they have venues like public baths for gay men, but there are no public baths for lesbians because we're poorer and there's not a big enough market."

Many of China's most committed women's rights activists outside the government system are lesbian. Li says that while women tend to be straight or uncertain about their sexual orientation at first, once they have become feminist activists they may begin to identify as lesbian, or at least as bisexual. She quotes a saying from her lesbian feminist friend Da Tu: "They go in straight and they come out bent." Although Li has long identified as lesbian, she believes that the political decision to engage in grassroots feminist activism in China causes women to think more radically about all aspects of their lives, including sexual orientation: "Feminism allows for more possibilities as a person; it lets women see that we can make a different kind of life choice." Also, Li argues that it's much easier for lesbians to break free of the "traditional binds of Chinese society." Those include, of course, intense pressure to enter into a heterosexual marriage.

Xu Bin is head of Tongyu, or 'Common Language', a grassroots rights group for lesbians, bisexual women and transgender people in China, founded in 2005. Xu, who is in her early forties, observes that there has been a gradual increase in the Chinese public's acceptance of the LGBTQ community since the government took homosexuality off its list of "mental diseases" in 2001. During Xu's first years in college in the 1990s, she had already had secret romantic relationships with women, but was unable to find any information that did not make her feel bad about her sexual identity:

> Homosexuality was not just a mental disease, but also a "hooligan crime." The definition of the crime was very vague, but any kind of "indecent behavior" could cause you to be expelled from your job, put in jail, or sent to a labor camp…. In college I knew homosexuality was very bad, horrible; you could be punished; you're a hooligan, a mad person – it was all bad and far from my world. I had a very difficult time trying to relate homosexuality to myself. Then, when I was in my last year in college, suddenly my school had basic Internet service – just basic news groups – but I found another world. Through the Internet, I got access to LGBT news groups, I don't know where they were from – the US or Europe – but it really opened the world for me and a lot of information came in.

After college, Xu Bin went to graduate school in the United States and became involved in various LGBTQ groups on campus: "Suddenly, all these things from the Internet and the books I read became real in my life." When Xu returned to Beijing, she continued her advocacy work for lesbians through a new, unregistered group started in 1998, called the "Beijing Sisters". It organized a lesbian culture festival in 2001, which was raided by the police. "The activists were detained and the whole group was crushed after that," says Xu.

Xu was able to set up the Tongyu group in 2005, which started out with lesbian community building:

> In Beijing, we have lesbian gatherings every week to talk about marriage pressure, coming out, coming out to oneself and how to deal with intimate relationships, and also with parents, family members; it's like a support group. We try to encourage individuals in different cities throughout China to set up similar groups. Grassroots groups are very important for lesbian, gay and bi people to reach out to the many people out there who are alone and are struggling.

Tongyu has since expanded its activities to embrace public education on LGBTQ issues and policy work on intimate partner violence and censorship of LGBTQ media. As with many other feminist grassroots groups, Tongyu has been unable to register either as an NGO or even as a commercial enterprise, despite many attempts over the years. This inability to register as an organization severely impedes the group's visibility and access to funding. Xu Bin explains: "Even for overseas funding, we need to have legal status – they can't fund organizations using personal bank accounts, so it's hard for us to raise money, to pay rent for an office building and the overheads for financial management."

LGBTQ websites are routinely targeted in "anti-pornography" media crackdowns. LGBTQ films are banned from being shown in public, and must be screened quietly in people's homes or non-public spaces. Still, Xu says that the popularity of social media like Weibo in recent years has created a vastly expanded online space for the LGBTQ community in China:

> Before, many people were kind of in the dark; they didn't have any access to LGBT information… But the Internet changed all that. For the first time, many people realized, "Oh, there are people like me." [LGBTQ] websites, underground films, magazines, and books may not have a license, but they still play an important role for gays, lesbians, and other sexual minorities in building an identity and empowering them.

In addition to having to cope with societal discrimination against the LGBTQ community, lesbian groups are marginalized by officially registered Chinese women's rights groups, including some NGOs. Xu points out that (at the time of writing) the All-China Women's Federation has rarely included work on lesbians or bisexual women because they are considered "too sensitive." Xu's group conducted a survey in 2009 on intimate partner violence against lesbian and bisexual women in eight cities, which found that the primary perpetrators of domestic violence were the *parents* of lesbian or bisexual daughters, and, secondly, intimate partners. While women's rights NGOs and lawyers are lobbying for the introduction of legislation on intimate partner violence, Tongyu has pushed for an acknowledgment that same-sex couples should also be protected from violence. Yet other women's groups tell Xu that without the imprimatur of the All-China Women's Federation, they do not dare raise issues related to lesbians.

Xu argues that lesbians in China are far less privileged than gay men, in general, which is why her group caters specifically to women who are lesbian, bisexual, or transgender:

> The media often use HIV and AIDS as a way to talk about gay issues, but lesbians are not so visible. Gay men sometimes argue that they have more pressure to marry and carry on the family line, so women are just tools [for them to marry], but that statement itself shows the gender inequality. Economically, women are more disadvantaged in general. Lesbians and transgender people in other places work more hand in hand with the women's rights movement, but this hasn't happened in China because we don't have a real women's rights movement; it's more about state-supported women's organizations that support very mainstream issues... Lesbians in mainland China have so few resources and not enough allies, unlike in Taiwan, where the women's rights movement is strong, and there is very strong advocacy for LGBT rights.

Activist Li Maizi is even more blunt: "We're happy to work with gay men who support gender equality, but some gay rights organizations oppose women, so why should we work with them?"

"Why would they oppose you?" I asked.

"Because they're men; they don't care that we're all queer," says Li. "Some gay men are very patriarchal, just look at all the *tongqi* [straight women unwittingly married to gay men] – I can't understand this, it's just corrupt morals!" says Li, referring to the fact that the majority of gay men in China are married to or will marry straight women, according to Zhang Beichuan of Qingdao University Medical School.

Li Maizi concedes that gay men are under pressure to enter into a heterosexual marriage (although, just as with straight men, it is far more socially acceptable for them to marry later than women.) But she says there's no excuse for deceiving women who are themselves under intense pressure to marry. "There are so many gay male QQ [chat] groups, saying, 'oh, I need to marry right now! It's time to find myself a wife!' It's all very easy for them to do," says Li.

Xu Bin points out that just as there is less funding for lesbian groups than for gay men, there are also far fewer studies of lesbians than of gay men in China. Gay marriage is still not legal, so in recent years, gay men and lesbians in big cities such as Beijing, Shanghai, and Guangzhou have started to marry each other in weddings of convenience or "functional marriages" (*xingshi hunyin*). In such arrangements, a gay man marries a lesbian in order to present a facade of heterosexual marriage to alleviate pressure from parents and extended families, while carrying out their "real" love life among their own circle of friends, often in another city. These "functional marriages" have become very popular in some LGBTQ circles. However, Xu Bin is wary:

> I myself wouldn't recommend it. I think it's a passing phase because of the great pressure people are under to get married... There are different ways to fight against the institution of heterosexual marriage. Some people – if they have resources and options – can remain single or in a same-sex relationship without pressure... But for many other people, they don't have those options, so their options are: you either marry a heterosexual spouse and hide your identity, or you try to marry someone who understands your situation and maybe needs your help... It's a good example of how marriage as an institution has nothing to do with romantic love.

Much more research needs to be carried out on "functional" marriages between a gay man and a lesbian. But it is possible that these marriages may result in the same kinds of unequal, gendered financial arrangements that are prevalent among heterosexual couples, such as relying on the woman's income and assets to help finance a "marital" home registered solely in the man's name.

The future of women's rights in China

When asked whether she is optimistic about the future of women's rights in China, Li Maizi replies, "I am an idealist, but I am not in a hurry to see real change."

Since the Chinese government imposes such tight restrictions on public demonstrations of any kind, Li's group has adopted a strategy of "low-profile group, high-profile content." She explains:

> All of our actions are launched by [relatively unknown] individuals, to avoid being labeled [politically] "sensitive." The authorities always want to know who the organizer is. But if there's no organizer, you have no idea who to arrest. So our actions are spontaneous... We don't have a prominent Internet presence, except for a couple of women's websites, but they're basically decoration, they're just put there for people to look at. We all look out for a message, and then we get together to plan an action; there's no organizer.

And, although Li Maizi frequently comments on Weibo addressing her thousands of followers, she says that social media are not the "primary battlefield" for her group:

> Weibo is very patriarchal. It's a platform for scolding and abusing women, so there's no way it can be used effectively to support women. Especially now, when there is still no widespread consciousness about citizens' rights yet. The people who like to comment on Weibo are mostly men, and these men tend to have no gender awareness at all. And women's time is eaten up by all their social and family obligations, like housework and childcare, and they don't like to speak out. So it's particularly difficult to use Weibo to mobilize women.

Since Li's group is not registered as a company, most of its activists are volunteers. "We want to challenge and deconstruct power, to build an equal society ... so we're very careful not to build up opinion leaders. We want to attract and create more and more feminist activists; we don't just want a few people to lead this movement," says Li.

Yet at the time of writing, the political space for women's rights activism – or any form of rights activism – appeared to have contracted. By December 2013, over a hundred activists had been detained or arrested that year on charges of "unlawful assembly" or, in some cases, "inciting subversion", according to human rights groups. One crackdown focused on the "New Citizens' Movement," a coalition of academics, lawyers, and liberals calling on Chinese officials to disclose their assets and curb corruption. Eva Pils, founding co-director of the Center for Rights and Justice at the Faculty of Law of the Chinese University of Hong Kong, told the *Telegraph* that the goal of the "New Citizens' Movement" was "to create a kind of civil society force that through solidarity is able to affect the political process, to bring about political change." Pils added that the group was set up as a "leaderless movement, which would be able to continue operating even if key figures were detained."

Since Li Maizi's group also uses the "leaderless movement" strategy, the crackdown on "New Citizens' Movement" members has had a chilling effect on her group's plans for future actions. "Beijing has been too repressive lately; other groups have been closed down, and we don't dare organize any actions for the time being," says Li. Yet government crackdowns ebb and flow, activists groups lie low for a while, then re-emerge with new initiatives.

"In the initial part of our social movements, the 'action' [protest] is very important, but it's easy to make noise. To push, push, push is very hard," says Li. "We have to turn to different forms of advocacy at different times." For example, although Li's group has staged some dramatic street "actions" addressing intimate partner violence in China, feminist lawyers and academics have worked behind the scenes for more than a decade to pass national legislation on domestic violence. As of November 2013, the legislation still had not been approved. Since the political environment is so repressive, for the time being Li and her colleagues have turned to survey research and letter writing rather than engaging in public street actions. Her group is now trying to come up with more effective strategies to fight for women's rights without increasing the political risk.

"It will require a very long, drawn-out period of struggle to see any progress, especially when it comes to gender issues," asserts Li. She is encouraged by the increase in Chinese society's acceptance of LGBTQ rights over the past decade and a half, but says that conservative attitudes toward women and families will take much longer to change. "I think that in about thirty years, we should be able to see some real change," says Li.

Meanwhile, many women have spoken or written to me about their private anger, which they feel unable to voice in public. Consider just a couple of comments posted to my Weibo account in July 2013:

> This kind of language [about "leftover" women] shows that there is a premeditated, organized effort both from above and from below to plunder, pillage and humiliate women. The tragedy is that Chinese women are not in a position to rebel.

> We don't even have human rights. How can we ask for women's rights?

Given the political risks involved in organizing an independent women's rights movement, some educated women are fighting back against gender discrimination on an individual level, by rejecting the institution of marriage. One university-educated woman in her mid-twenties spoke at length about her frustration after attending one of my talks on "leftover" women at Yiyuan Gongshe, an informal space for activists and academics in Beijing. During the question–and–answer period, the young woman explained why she is exercising a deliberate choice to stay single:

> My strongest emotion is anger. The government has inserted itself into the tiniest, most minute details of an individual's life… All of a sudden I have the feeling that everyone around me – my mother, all my elders, my grandmothers on both sides – suddenly become really worried about my not being married… The scariest thing is that individual matters are so controlled by official power, by the power of the state… plus the enduring values of patriarchal culture. These forms of power all hurt women. So I'm extremely angry. You really shouldn't enter into that trap; you need to find a way out. The institution of marriage basically benefits men… The most rational choice is to stay single.

Another young woman offered the following response to my June 2013 talk in Beijing:

> Women's investment in the marriage is invisible… The woman's duty is to take care of the child, take care of the elderly, give birth to the child, do the housework – these burdens are all taken for granted. Hardly anyone thinks that these are the man's obligations. This is so unfair… Nowadays, many urban men don't want the woman just to stay at home not making any money and being a housewife. Men demand that the woman brings her income to the marriage and invests it with him… She brings her income, she brings her assets, she makes the man feel very safe and secure, she gives the man a long and satisfying sex life, she gives birth to a child who bears the man's last name. So this is why officials are putting so much energy into spreading propaganda about "leftover" women. Many women who aren't thinking clearly are dragged into this kind of married life. If it weren't for the propaganda, a lot of loser men [*diaosinan*] would never be able to find a woman willing to marry them.

In Shanghai, one 26-year-old university graduate told me flatly that she refuses to marry because "marriage in China is a living hell." She has formed close friendships with other like-minded women in Shanghai, who support each other in rejecting the intense family and societal pressure to marry.

Statistical data at the time of writing show that, unlike many women in neighboring East Asian and Southeast Asian countries who are choosing to stay single, few women in China are rejecting marriage altogether. Recent studies, such as the 2013 paper "Coming of Age in Times of Change: The Transition to Adulthood in China" by sociologists Wei-Jun Jean Yeung and Shu Hu, show that 30 to 40 percent of Chinese agree that "a bad marriage is better than being single," based on their analysis of the Chinese General Social Survey of 2005–08. China's 2010 census reported that the average marriage age for a woman was still only 24.9, up slightly from 23.4 in 2000.

Yet statistics are often slow to reflect rapid social changes on the ground. It is possible that the ideas of some of the single, educated, urban women I have interviewed will increasingly take hold in large cities across China. Population specialists Wang Feng and Cai Yong, who have analyzed marriage trends in Shanghai, detect a possible long-term move away from the traditional model of universal marriage. In a paper on the "(re) emergence of late marriage in new Shanghai," Wang and Cai predict the following:

> At least for the highly educated women in Shanghai, almost 7 percent will remain single at age 45 if the marriage trend observed in the decade of 1996–2005 continues. With the rapid expansion of China's high education, especially women's education, if this trend of non-marriage continues, China will soon face a marriage revolution just like what has happened in many developed countries.

While some women deliberately renounce marriage, others

are simply embracing their single lifestyles and finding ways to ignore the omnipresent pressure to marry.

Lan Fang is a 32-year-old client-relations manager for a financial company in Shanghai. After graduating from college, Lan went on to get a master's degree in English from a prestigious university in Beijing, then moved to Shanghai, where she now earns a very comfortable income of RMB 20,000 a month (around US$3,200), well above the average monthly pay there. "Where I grew up in Nanjing, I saw so many couples getting into big fights, and most of them seemed unhappy. Plus, so many men have affairs," says Lan. She has thought about maybe marrying one day if she finds a partner who could really make her happy, but she is loath to give up the freedoms she enjoys. Her typical schedule includes going out with friends in the evening for dinner, and perhaps to a movie or a concert; working out several times a week at the gym; reading novels; and taking French classes on Saturdays "just for fun."

The only thing Lan regrets about her single status is that the Shanghai government tightened restrictions on single people buying homes in 2012, such that residents who do not possess a Shanghai *hukou* must be married in order to buy property (see Chapter 3). Lan has a Beijing *hukou*, so she is not permitted to buy an apartment in Shanghai. Still, she believes the government restrictions on buying property will loosen by the time she turns 40. "I want to buy a place where I can take shelter in my old age. The population is shrinking, so I'll probably be able to buy an apartment of my own later in life [assuming property purchasing restrictions are lifted]." In the meantime, Lan is spending only a small fraction of her income on the monthly rent of RMB 2,000 for an apartment she shares with two friends near her office in downtown Shanghai. And she scoffs at the question of whether she might ever marry a man in order to own a home or achieve a sense of security. "Of course not! My life in Shanghai now is very rich, why would I want to change it?" she retorts.

Like many other single women over 30, Lan has to endure pressure from her family and colleagues, and insults from the media, but she has learned to shrug it all off: "This is just gender discrimination and I don't pay attention anymore."

Acknowledgments

To the women and men who opened your hearts to me in our long conversations, thank you for trusting in me and allowing me to record some incredibly intimate details of your private lives. I hope that I have sufficiently protected your identities and not caused too much trouble. To all who agreed to use your real names in interviews with me, I am especially grateful and in awe of your extraordinary commitment to women's rights: Feng Yuan, Kim Lee, Li Maizi, Li Ying, Xu Bin, and Zeng Jinyan.

I thank my professors at Tsinghua University's Department of Sociology for supporting my research from its earliest stages. My Ph.D. supervisor, Liu Jingming, offered me invaluable guidance from the beginning of my graduate program and gave me critical feedback throughout my years of data gathering and analysis. Shen Yuan, Jing Jun, Li Qiang, Guo Yuhua, Luo Jar-der, Jean-Louis Rocca, and Aurore Merle helped me hone my arguments with their intelligent critiques. Thanks to my classmates in our sociology graduate seminars, who energetically discussed my research ideas. I also thank the China Scholarship Council for supporting my graduate studies.

I am profoundly grateful to Lydia H. Liu – my undergraduate thesis supervisor at Harvard University – and to Rebecca E. Karl for their enthusiastic support from very early on in my research.

They helped buoy my spirits during some difficult times along the way, and I was inspired by their excellent book, edited with Dorothy Ko, *The Birth of Chinese Feminism: Essential Texts in Transnational Theory.*

I am indebted to Ching Kwan Lee, who taught one of my graduate seminars as a visiting professor at Tsinghua in 2010 and gave me valuable suggestions when I first came up with the germ of my research idea. I also thank her and Alvin Y. So for inviting me to present some of my findings at the 2012 Hong Kong University of Science and Technology International Conference on "Class, Power and China," where I benefited greatly from everyone's feedback. Fred Block, whom I met at the conference, very generously critiqued several drafts of a paper I wrote on "leftover" women and residential real-estate wealth, which helped me frame my argument much more effectively. I thank the Hong Kong University of Science and Technology Social Science Division for giving me additional support as I finish my Ph.D. program.

I was extremely fortunate to have Sarah Schafer extensively edit many of my book chapters. Her incisive comments significantly sharpened my writing. I also thank the following scholars for providing very helpful critiques of my work: Kathryn Bernhardt, Angie Baecker, Donald Clarke, Marta Elliott, Shirlena Huang, Joya Misra, Eileen Otis, Hugh Shapiro, Adia Harvey Wingfield and Suowei Xiao. I am especially grateful to Jeffrey Wasserstrom for inviting me to write an essay for *Dissent* magazine, which evolved into several parts of this book, and for supporting my work so much. I thank *Dissent* executive editor Maxine Phillips for her enthusiasm for my article "Women's Rights at Risk," published in the Spring 2013 issue. I deeply appreciate Li Yuan's offer to publish a Chinese translation of my *Ms. Magazine* "leftover" women op-ed for the *Wall Street Journal* Chinese website. That received a tremendous response and dramatically broadened my dialogue on Weibo with women throughout China. Thanks to those who ably translated my commentaries on women for the *New York Times* Chinese website. I also thank Ying Zhu for translating my *Dissent* essay into Chinese and Marie-Hélène Corbin for translating it into French.

I was very inspired by the exchanges I had with lawyers and scholars at the 2012 International Conference on Feminism and the Law in Pune, India – in particular, Jaya Sagade, Flavia Agnes, and Mokshda Pertaub Bhushan. I also received helpful feedback at other conferences, including the dissertation reading group of the Tsinghua–Columbia Center for Translingual and Transcultural Studies in Beijing; the workshop "Contemporary Research on Chinese Women" in Beijing, organized by the French Centre for Research on Contemporary China (CEFC); the Association for Asian Studies annual meeting in San Diego; the "Feminists Face the State" symposium at U.C. Berkeley; the Sociologists for Women in Society and Association of Black Sociologists Student Roundtable at the American Sociological Association annual meeting in Denver; the American Sociological Association Sexualities mini-conference in Denver; and the Hong Kong Sociological Association annual meeting.

Many thanks to members of Sociologists for Women in Society who gave me advice and encouragement, in particular Amy Brainer, Tressie McMillan Cottom, Jeanne Flavin, Laura Kramer, Stephanie Nawyn, and Nancy Naples. I am grateful to Ted Glasser, my journalism professor at Stanford University, who ignited my interest in becoming a professional journalist.

I also thank the Beijing International Society, Bill Bikales, Julia Broussard, Melindah Bush, Chen Yiyun, Jeremy Goldkorn, Elizabeth Haenle, David Moser, Meir Shahar, Hsiu-hua Shen, Kristie Lu Stout, Jon Sullivan, Didi Kirsten Tatlow, Nora Tejada, Tong Xin, Sebastian Veg, Brian Zittel, Xiao Hang, and the wonderful volunteers at Yiyuan Gongshe in Beijing. A huge thank you to Zed Books Asian Arguments editor Paul French for approaching me to write this book and for all of his intelligent (and often very entertaining) comments. I also thank Zed Books commissioning editor Kim Walker and foreign rights director Renata Kasprzak.

I am indebted to my mother, Beverly Hong-Fincher, for raising me bilingually in Chinese and English. She encouraged me to embark on a Chinese-language Ph.D. program in Beijing, which seemed crazy at first for an American like me, but turned out to be a valuable educational experience. I wish that my father, John Fincher, were still here to read this book. He taught me how to observe the world and take notes whenever I had an interesting thought. I would have loved to share my discoveries with him. I thank my brother, Hanson, for being there for me when I most needed his support. I thank my children, Aidan and Liam, for bringing me joy and lightness.

Many thanks to everyone who interacts with me on Twitter and Weibo. You have supported me through some very lonely and frustrating times in front of my computer.

Finally, I thank Mike Forsythe, my most conscientious editor and my greatest champion. You cheered me on whenever I doubted myself. I am so grateful to have you by my side.

Notes

NB   Chinese state media websites are constantly deleting posts, so I have provided only some of the relevant hyperlinks.

INTRODUCTION

3   *That same year...*: "2006 nian wo guo yüyan wenzi you you 'xin miankong'." Ministry of Education. August 17, 2007.

3   *Typical headlines...*: "'Huangjin shengnü' 4 da xinli zhangai." Xinhua. September 10, 2013.

3   *Eight Simple...*: "Jiandan 8 zhao cong 'shengnü' zhong tuwei." Xinhua. May 21, 2010.

3   *Do Leftover Women Really...*: "You duoshao shengnü zhende zhide women tongqing?" Published March 14, 2011 on Women's Federation website. My *New York Times* op-ed of October, 12, 2012, "China's 'Leftover' Women," criticized the Women's Federation for insulting single Chinese women and quoted two excerpts from the above column. The *New York Times* Chinese website published my op-ed on October 15, 2012 as "Weihe zhongguo fulian dui 'shengnü' weiyan songting." The Chinese op-ed circulated on Weibo and sparked an outcry by women. Two months later the Women's Federation website deleted this and many other columns about *shengnü*.

4   *The irony...*: "Zhonggong zhongyang guowuyuan guanyu quanmian jiaqiang renkou he jihuashengyu gongzuo tongchou jiejue renkou wenti de jueding." [State Council Decision on Fully Enhancing the Population and Family Planning Program and Comprehensively Addressing Population Issues] Xinhua. January 22, 2007 (http://news.xinhuanet.com/politics/2007–01/22/content_5637713.htm; accessed November 6, 2013).

4   *The official Communist...*: "30 sui yixia nanxing bi nüxing duo liangqian duo wan; shengnan shi ge da wenti." Xinhua. June 21, 2012.

5   *On the contrary...*: Figure from Zhang Zhi Ming, Dilip Shahani, and Keith Chan, "China's Housing Concerns," in *HSBC Global Research Report*, June 7, 2010, p. 5. The value of China's residential real estate surpassed 3.27 times China's GDP, at RMB 109 trillion, in February 2010.

5   *That amounted to...*: Ibid. Based on 3.3 times China's GDP at the end of 2013, or RMB 187.7 trillion, which is equivalent to US$30.69 trillion.

5   *Chinese consumers…*: Deborah Davis, "Who Gets The House? Renegotiating Property Rights in Post-Socialist Urban China." *Modern China* 36 (5) (2010): 463–92.

7   *Then in August 2011…*: "Zui gao renmin fayuan guanyu shiyong 'Zhonghua Renmin Gongheguo Hunyinfa' ruogan wenti de jieshi (san)." Supreme People's Court. August 13, 2011 (www.court.gov.cn/qwfb/sfjs/201108/ t20110815_159794.htm; accessed November 7, 2013).

7   *According to a 2012…*: "Wo de hun yu fang." Horizon China. October 29, 2012.

8   *Curious about…*: My Weibo account is @洪理达 tsinghua.

9   *Almost two-thirds…*: Wang Feng, Yong Cai, and Baochang Gu, "Population, Policy and Politics: How Will History Judge China's One-Child Policy?" *Population and Development Review* 38 (Supplement) 2012: 115–29.

10 *In other, wealthier…*: Wei-Jun Jean Yeung and Cheryll Alipio, "Transitioning to Adulthood in Asia: School, Work, and Family Life." *ANNALS of the American Academy of Political and Social Science* 646 (2013): 6–27.

10 *In mainland…*: Wei-Jun Jean Yeung and Shu Hu, "Coming of Age in Times of Change: The Transition to Adulthood in China." *ANNALS of the American Academy of Political and Social Science* 646 (2013): 149–71.

13 *But in 1907…*: Louise Edwards, *Gender, Politics and Democracy: Women's Suffrage in China*. Stanford CA: Stanford University Press, 2008, p. 62.

ONE

15 *Chen has taken to heart…*: "Wan hun nü buneng yiwei 'wan' xiaqu." Xinhua. November 18, 2008.

16 *In 2010…*: "Diaocha cheng guoren xuan banlü ai wending." Xinhua. December 16, 2010.

16 *The widely circulated…*: Sub-heading: "Kankan ni 'sheng' daole na yi ji" in ibid.

17 *Other, supposedly…*: "Xinhua Insight: China's 'Leftover Women' Unite This Singles Day." *China Daily*. November 10, 2011.

17 *Over the years…*: Esther Ngan-Ling Chow, Naihua Zhang, and Jinling Wang, "Promising and Contested Fields: Women's Studies and Sociology of Women/ Gender in Contemporary China." *Gender & Society* 18 (2) (2004): 161–88.

18 *When the Communist Party…*: Rebecca E. Karl, *Mao Zedong in the Twentieth Century World: A Concise History*. Durham NC: Duke University Press, 2010.

18 *Under the Party's…*: Susan Greenhalgh, "Fresh Winds in Beijing: Chinese Feminists Speak Out on the One-Child Policy and Women's Lives." *Signs* 26 (3) (2001): 847–86.

18 *Literary critic…*: Lydia H. Liu, "Invention and Intervention: The Female Tradition in Modern Chinese Literature." In Tani E. Barlow (ed.), *Gender Politics in Modern China: Writing & Feminism*. Durham NC: Duke University Press, 1993; Tani E. Barlow, "Theorizing Woman: *Funü, guojia, jiating*." *Genders* 10 (Spring 1991): 132–60.

18 *In fact, the peculiarity…*: Thanks to Jeffrey Wasserstrom for this insight.

18 *Take this Xinhua…*: "Jiandan 8 zhao cong 'shengnü' zhong tuwei." Xinhua. May 21, 2010.

20 *And once a woman…*: See also Suowei Xiao, "The 'Second-Wife' Phenomenon and the Relational Construction of Class-Coded Masculinities in Contemporary China." *Men and Masculinities* 14 (5) (2011): 607–27.

20 *Consider this Xinhua…*: "Yingdui hunyin weiji nüren yao xuehui shanbian." Published on ACWF website on June 20, 2011; deleted in December 2012.

20 *The country's sex…*: "Sex Ratio May Cause Marriage Squeeze." Xinhua. August 24, 2013. See also Valerie M. Hudson and Andrea Den Boer. *Bare Branches: The Security Implications of Asia's Surplus Male Population.* Cambridge MA: MIT Press, 2004.

21 *Other countries with a high…*: UNFPA Asia and the Pacific Regional Office. "Sex Imbalances at Birth: Current Trends, Consequences and Policy Implications." August 2013.

21 *In June, 2012…*: "30 sui yixia nanxing bi nüxing duo liangqian duo wan; shengnan shi ge da wenti." Xinhua. June 21, 2012.

22 *Mara…*: Mara Hvistendahl, *Unnatural Selection: Choosing Boys over Girls, and the Consequences of a World Full of Men.* New York: Public Affairs, 2011.

22 *The matchmaking…*: "Zhongguo 'shengnan' yanjiu baogao: 'langduo roushao' – shengnan biaoshi wu yali." *People's Daily.* March 14, 2013.

23 *As any Communist…*: E.g. "Yi hexie jiating jianshe cujin shehui hexie." *People's Daily.* May 17, 2010.

23 *China's president from 2003 to 2013…*: Susan L. Shirk, *China: Fragile Superpower.* Oxford: Oxford University Press, 2008.

23 *Tsinghua University…*: Shen Yuan, Guo Yuhua and Sun Liping. "'Weiwen' xin silu: liyi biaoda zhiduhua, shixian changzhijiu an." April 15, 2010. *Nanfang Zhoumo* (www.infzm.com/content/43853; accessed November 24, 2013).

23 *One of the report's…*: E.g. Sun's estimate cited in Feng Shu, "A National Conundrum." *People's Daily.* February 10, 2012.

23 *In 2013…*: B. Blanchard and J. Ruwitch. "China Hikes Defense Budget, to Spend More on Internal Security." Reuters. March 5, 2013.

24 *Brook Larmer reports…*: B. Larmer, "China's Arranged Remarriages." *New York Times.* May 9, 2010.

24 *Women who have…*: J. Kaiman, "China's Unmarried Mothers Could Face Huge Fines." *Guardian.* June 3, 2013.

24 *These illustrations…*: Search Google Images 剩女 [*shengnü*] for most recent illustrations.

25 *Almost 26 percent1…*: ACWF and NBS Survey. "Di san qi zhongguo funü shehui diwei diaocha zhuyao shuju baogao." Executive report in *Funü yanjiu lun cong* 6 (108) (2011): 5–15.

25 *Record numbers…*: E. Zlomek, "Women are Taking the GMAT in Record Numbers." *Businessweek.* March 5, 2013.

25 *Women now outnumber…*: Ministry of Education cited in "Women College

Students Continue to Outnumber Male Peers." Women's Federation website. November 7, 2013.

26   *The caption above her...*: E.g. Nanfang dushi bao, "Baima wangzi zenme hai bu chuxian? Zai deng xiaqu, baixue gongzhu dou cheng laowupo le." 2012 website link deleted, but image accessible on other websites.

26   *The tower...*: "Gao xueli, gao zhiwei, gao shouru."

28   *I believe it is no...*: [2007 State Council Decision...] Ibid.

28   *The State Council... "*: E.g. "Guanyu guanche shishi 'zhonggong zhongyang guowuyuan guanyu quanmian jiaqiang renkou he jihua shengyu gongzuo tongchou jiejue renkou wenti de jueding' de shishi." E.g. Songyang government website. August 13, 2007.

29   *Anthropologist Ellen...*: Ellen Judd, *The Chinese Women's Movement between State and Market*. Stanford CA: Stanford University Press, 2002.

29   *As cultural studies...*: Harriet Evans, "Past, Perfect or Imperfect: Changing Images of the Ideal Wife." In Susan Brownell and Jeffrey N. Wasserstrom (eds), *Chinese Femininities/Chinese Masculinities*. Berkeley: University of California Press, 2002, pp. 348, 358.

29   *Demographers Susan...*: Susan Greenhalgh and Edwin W. Winckler, *Governing China's Population: From Leninist to Neoliberal Biopolitics*. Stanford CA: Stanford University Press, 2005.

30   *The eugenics campaign...*: Susan Greenhalgh, *Cultivating Global Citizens: Population in the Rise of China*. Cambridge MA: Harvard University Press, 2010, p. 58.

30   *But in neighboring Japan...*: Gavin W. Jones and Bina Gubhaju, "Factors Influencing Changes in Mean Age at First Marriage and Proportions Never Marrying in the Low-Fertility Countries of East and Southeast Asia." *Asian Population Studies* 5 (3) (2009): 237–65.

30   *Since 2008...*: "Nanjing 'chengshi shengnü' xianxiang riyi yanzhong – jishengwei zhunbei ganyu." *Jinling Wanbao*. December 2, 2008; "Ningbo weihe duo 'shengnü'?" *Ningbo Wanbao*. June 21, 2012.

31   *Local Women's...*: "Shi fulian jianli 'women xiangyue ba' – xinxi gongxiang pingtai wei 'shengnü' dang hongniang." *Pinghu Fuxun* 3 (March 2012): 17.

31   *Since 2011...*: "Shanghai xiangqin dahui xiyin siwan ren ruchang." Xinhua. May 21, 2013.

31   *Xinhua News ran...*: "Jinnian wanren xiangqinhui sancheng nüsheng shi '90 hou' – baoming jiezhi ben zhouwu." Xinhua. May 7, 2013.

31   *Moreover, government-sponsored...*: "Matchmaking Fair Held in Hangzhou." Xinhua. November 2, 2013.

32   *The official People's Daily...*: "Shuju xianshi: Beijing quexian er meinian chusheng 4000 yu ming." *People's Daily*. September 16, 2013.

32   *A related report...*: "China Sees 900,000 Newborns with Birth Defects Annually." Xinhua. September 12, 2012.

32   *Scientists...*: Aiguo Ren, Xinghua Qiu, Lei Jin, Jin Ma, Zhiwen Li, Le Zhang,

Huiping Zhu, Richard H. Finnell, and Tong Zhu. "Association of Selected Persistent Organic Pollutants in the Placenta with the Risk of Neural Tube Defects." *Proceedings of the National Academy of Sciences of the United States of America* 108 (31) (2011): 12770–75; C. Larson, "Air Pollution, Birth Defects, and the Risk in China (and Beyond)." *Businessweek*. March 28, 2013.

33 *Susan Greenhalgh…*: Greenhalgh, *Cultivating Global Citizens*, p. 26.

34 *The increased educational…*: E.g. Vanessa L. Fong, "China's One-Child Policy and the Empowerment of Urban Daughters." *American Anthropologist* 104 (4) (2002): 1098–109.

34 *In just one…*: D.K. Tatlow, "Women in China Face Rising University Entry Barriers." October 8, 2012.

35 *China's gender income…*: E.g. Philip N. Cohen and Wang Feng, "Market and Gender Pay Equity: Have Chinese Reforms Narrowed the Gap?" In Deborah S. Davis and Wang Feng (eds), *Creating Wealth and Poverty in Postsocialist China*, Stanford CA: Stanford University Press, 2009.

36 *But by 2010…*: Isabelle Attané, "Being a Woman in China Today: A Demography of Gender." *China Perspectives* 4 (2012): 5–16.

36 *China's 2010 census…*: ibid.

36 *The figure stacks…*: Francine D. Blau and Lawrence M. Kahn, "Female Labor Supply: Why is the US Falling Behind?" NBER Working Paper No. 18702. January 2013.

36 *China's urban employment…*: Population Census Office and NBS. "Zhongguo 2010 nian renkou pucha ziliao." Beijing: China Statistics Press, 2012.

36 *The 2010 rate…*: See graph in Attané, "Being a Woman in China Today," p. 8.

37 *The decline…*: Yongping Jiang, "Employment and Chinese Urban Women under Two Systems." In Zheng Bijun, Tao Jie and Shirley L. Mow (eds), *Holding Up Half the Sky: Chinese Women Past, Present, and Future*. New York: Feminist Press, 2004.

37 *Women were fired…*: Liu Jieyu, *Gender and Work in Urban China: Women Workers of the Unlucky Generation*. London: Routledge, 2007.

37 *The fall in labor force…*: Liu Jingming, "Laodongli shichang jiegou bianqian yu renli ziben shouyi." *Shehuixue yanjiu* 6 (2006).

38 *A "Women Return…"*: Tong Xin, "Sanshi nian Zhongguo nüxing/xingbie shehuixue yanjiu." *Funü yanjiu luncong* 3 (86) (2008): 69.

38 *Service employers…*: Eileen Otis, *Markets and Bodies: Women, Service Work, and the Making of Inequality in China*. Stanford CA: Stanford University Press, 2012, p. 36.

39 *Although women…*: Wang Zheng. "Gender, Employment, and Women's Resistance." In Elizabeth J. Perry and Mark Selden (eds), *Chinese Society: Change, Conflict and Resistance*, 2nd edn, London: Routledge, 2003, p. 159.

41 *Moreover, China's National…*: "Zhongguo nannü hunlian guan diaocha: 18 – 25 sui nüxing – 70% shi dashukong." Xinhua. December 25, 2012.

42 *The Xinhua…*: "8 zhong nüren yi cheng shengnü – nanren yijian jiu xiang pao." *People's Daily* website. November 12, 2013.

42   *The Xinhua News website…*: "'Nü boshi' yu 'youfang shengnü'." April 27, 2013.

43   *It has intensified…*: Sandy To, "Understanding Sheng Nu ('Leftover Women'): The Phenomenon of Late Marriage among Chinese Professional Women." *Symbolic Interaction* 36 (1) (2013): 1–20.

TWO

44   *On the face of it…*: See my article "Women's Rights at Risk" in *Dissent*, Spring 2013 (www.dissentmagazine.org/article/womens-rights-at-risk).

45   *Even with tight…*: "China Home Ownership Reaches 90 Percent." Figure cited in *Economic Observer* online. May 16, 2012.

46   *A 2012 Horizon…*: Horizon China. October 29, 2012.

46   *At the time of writing, I had not…*: ACWF and NBS Survey, "Di san qi zhongguo funü shehui diwei diaocha zhuyao shuju baogao." Executive report in *Funü yanjiu lun cong* 6 (108) (2010): 5–15.

46   *A 2010 China research…*: Zhang Zhi Ming, Dilip Shahani, and Keith Chan, "China's Housing Concerns." HSBC Global Research Report. June 7, 2010, p. 5.

47   *The 2011 interpretation…*: "Zui gao renmin fayuan guanyu shiyong 'Zhonghua Renmin Gongheguo Hunyinfa' ruogan wenti de jieshi (san)." Supreme People's Court. August 13, 2011 (www.court.gov.cn/qwfb/sfjs/201108/t20110815_159794.htm; accessed November 7, 2013).

47   *This may be…*: Policies have "gender-specific consequences." See Joya Misra and Leslie King, "Women, Gender, and State Policies." In Thomas Janoski, Robert Alford, Alexander Hicks, and Mildred A. Schwartz (eds), *The Handbook of Political Sociology: States, Civil Societies, and Globalization*. New York: Cambridge University Press, 2005, p. 527.

47   *"This is a man's… "*: Li Ying, "Wo kan hunyinfa sifa jieshi san." August 8, 2011.

48   *Studies find…*: E.g. Kam Wah Chan and Fung Yi Chan, "Inclusion or Exclusion? Housing Battered Women in Hong Kong." *Critical Social Policy* 23 (4) (2003): 526–46.

48   *Official statistics…*: ACWF and NBS Survey, "Di san qi zhongguo funü shehui diwei diaocha zhuyao shuju baogao."

51   *Victor Yuan…*: Yuan summarized his findings at a media event in Beijing. Horizon China. October 29, 2012.

53   *In December 2010…*: "Diaocha cheng guoren xuan banlü ai wending." Xinhua. December 16, 2010.

53   *In a write-up…*: "Diaocha xianshi qicheng nüxing renwei nanfang bixu you fang cai jiehun." *People's Daily* website. December 16, 2010.

53   *I obtained the 2010…*: "2010 niandu quan guo hunlian diaocha sheji fangan." Main Organizer: China Marriage and Family Research Organization (affiliated to ACWF).

54   *At the end of 2011…*: "Piaozi, fangzi de jiujie – jiedu '2011 zhongguoren hunlian zhuangkuang diaocha baogao'." Xinhua. January 4, 2012.

55   *Horizon Chairman…*:Yuan spoke at a media event in Beijing. Horizon China. October 29, 2012.

55   *Curiously, China's National…*: "Zhongguo nannü hunlian guan diaocha…" Xinhua. December 25, 2012.

59   *Sociologist Mariko Lin Chang…*: Mariko Lin Chang, *Shortchanged: Why Women Have Less Wealth and What Can Be Done about It*. Oxford: Oxford University Press, 2010.

60   *Anthropologist Li Zhang…*: Li Zhang, *In Search of Paradise: Middle-Class Living in a Chinese Metropolis*. Ithaca NY: Cornell University Press, 2010, p. 168.

65   *Many studies…*: Arlie Russell Hochschild, *The Second Shift*. New York: Penguin Books, 1989;Veronica Jaris Tichenor, *Earning More and Getting Less:Why Successful Wives Can't Buy Equality*. New Brunswick: Rutgers University Press, 2005.

67   *The 2010 government…*: "Guowuyuan guanyu jianjue ezhi bufen chengshi fangjia guokuai shangzhang de tongzhi." State Council. April 17, 2010 (www.gov.cn/zwgk/2010–04/17/content_1584927.htm; accessed November 21, 2013).

68   *Consider that…*: ACWF and NBS Survey, "Di san qi zhongguo funü shehui diwei diaocha zhuyao shuju baogao."

68   *Yet studies…*: Zuo Jiping and Bian Yanjie. "Gendered Resources, Division of Housework, and Perceived Fairness – Case in Urban China." *Journal of Marriage and Family* 63 (4) (2001): 1122–33; Attané, "Being a Woman in China Today."

68   *Mariko Lin Chang…*: Chang, *Shortchanged*.

73   The insights…: Judith Butler, "Merely Cultural." *New Left Review* I/227, January–February 1998.

THREE

76   *China's hukou…*: Martin King Whyte, *One Country, Two Societies: Rural–Urban Inequality in Contemporary China*. Cambridge MA: Harvard University Press, 2010, p. 11.

76   *As part of China's privatization…*: Kam Wing Chan and Li Zhang. "The *Hukou* System and Rural–Urban Migration in China: Processes and Changes." *China Quarterly* 160 (1999): 818–55.

76   *When home prices…*: Fei-Ling Wang, "Reformed Migration Control and New Targeted People: China's Hukou System in the 2000s." *China Quarterly* 177 (2004): 115–32.

78   *My research…*: See also Shang-Jin Wei and Xiaobo Zhang, "The Competitive Saving Motive: Evidence from Rising Sex Ratios and Savings Rates in China." *Journal of Political Economy* 119 (3) (2011): 511–64.

80   *My findings…*: ACWF and NBS Survey, "Di san qi zhongguo funü shehui diwei diaocha zhuyao shuju baogao."

81   *Demographer Wang…*: Wang Feng, "Bringing an End to a Senseless Policy – China's 'One-Child' Rule Should be Scrapped." *New York Times*. November 19, 2013.

81 *Moreover, even before…*: Wang Feng, Yong Cai, and Baochang Gu, "Population, Policy and Politics: How Will History Judge China's One-Child Policy?" *Population and Development Review* 38 (Supplement) 2012: 115–29.

82 *Anthropologist Wang…*: Danning Wang, "Intergenerational Transmission of Family Property and Family Management in Urban China." In Harriet Evans and Julia C. Strauss (eds), *Gender in Flux: Agency and Its Limits in Contemporary China*, China Quarterly Special Issues New Series, No. 10. Cambridge: Cambridge University Press, 2011, p. 155.

84 *Urban home ownership…*: Li Zhang, *In Search of Paradise.*

85 *Zhang Yin's household…*: "Beijing luoshi guowuyuan fangdichan tiaokong 15 tiao xize." Xinhua. February 16, 2011.

85 *As the CEO…*: Li Guoping of Gaoce fangdichan guwen gongsi spoke at a Horizon media event, Beijing, October 29, 2012.

89 *New government…*: "Shanghai waidiren danshen maifang xinzheng." SouFun. October 17, 2012.

92 *I couldn't help…*: Zhang Beichuan's study cited in "Millions of Wives Wed to Gay Men: Expert." *China Daily.* February 2, 2013.

92 *In 1980…*: Ya Ping Wang and Alan Murie, "The Process of Commercialisation of Urban Housing in China." *Urban Studies* 33 (6) (1996): 971–89.

93 *Sociologist Ching Kwan Lee…*: Ching Kwan Lee, *Against the Law: Labor Protests in China's Rustbelt and Sunbelt.* Berkeley: University of California Press, 2007, p. 24.

93 *Many studies…*: Joyce Yanyun Man, Siqi Zheng, and Rongrong Ren, "Housing Policy and Housing Markets: Trends, Patterns and Affordability." In Joyce Yanyun Man (ed.), *China's Housing Reform and Outcomes.* Cambridge MA: Lincoln Institute of Land Policy, 2011.

93 *A 2012 survey…*: Horizon China, ibid.

93 *By another measure…*: IMF, CEIC, and Demographia cited in C. Rampell, "A Place that Makes New York Real Estate Look Cheap." *New York Times.* January 25, 2013.

93 *Yet, as noted…*: *Economic Observer* online, May 16, 2012.

93 *Sociologist Sun…*: Liping Sun, "Gao fangjia yu dangdai zhongguo shehui jiegou." *Changjiang zazhi.* July 25, 2007.

93 *The heavy parental…*: Y. Wang, "Beijing shouci goufang renqun pingjun nianling jin 27 sui." Xinhua. January 22, 2013.

94 *Property ownership…*: E.g. Luigi Tomba, "The Housing Effect: The Making of China's Social Distinctions." In Cheng Li (ed.), *China's Emerging Middle Class.* Washington DC: Brookings Institution Press, 2010.

95 *Sociologist Pierre…*: Pierre Bourdieu, *The Social Structures of the Economy.* Cambridge: Polity Press, 2005, p. 16.

95 *Property consultant…*: Li Guoping spoke at a Horizon media event, Beijing, October 29, 2012.

96 *One Beijing-based…*: Interviewed several times in 2011 and 2012.

96   *Isolated homeowner…*: E. Fung, "Shanghai Homeowners Smash Showroom in Protest over Falling Prices." *Wall Street Journal*. October 25, 2011.

96   *In another example…*: Y. Gu "Bringing Down 'Watch Brother': China's Online Corruption Busters Tread a Fine Line." *Time*. October 10, 2012.

97   *China's Central…*: China Digital Times, "Regulation and Control of the Real Estate Market." February 10, 2011 (http://chinadigitaltimes.net/2011/02/latest-directives-from-the-ministry-of-truth-february-10-15-2011; accessed November 22, 2013); China Digital Times, "A General Notice from the Central Propaganda Bureau Regarding News and Propaganda in 2011." January 13, 2011 (http://chinadigitaltimes.net/2011/01/2011-general-notice-from-the-central-propagandabureau; accessed November 22, 2013).

97   *Moody's Analytics…*: Michael Hendrix, "Three Reasons Why Household Formation is a Key Indicator of Economic Growth." US Chamber of Commerce website. November 15, 2012.

98   *For example, Sina…*: "2012 quanguo wanren hunfang guan da diaocha." February 13, 2012.

99   *Economists…*: Jonas D.M. Fisher and Martin Gervais, "Why Has Home Ownership Fallen among the Young?" *International Economic Review* 52 (3) (2011): 883–912.

100 *Nobel prize…*: Amartya K. Sen, "From Income Inequality to Economic Inequality." *Southern Economic Journal* 64 (2) (1997): 383–401.

101 *In Myth of…*: Martin King Whyte, *Myth of the Social Volcano: Perceptions of Inequality and Distributive Injustice in Contemporary China*. Stanford CA: Stanford University Press, 2010, p. 182.

101 *Sociologist Ching Kwan Lee…*: Ching Kwan Lee, "From Inequality to Inequity: Popular Conceptions of Social (In) justice in Beijing." In Deborah S. Davis and Wang Feng (eds), *Creating Wealth and Poverty in Postsocialist China*. Stanford CA: Stanford University Press, 2009, p. 228.

102 *Sociologist Jean-Louis Rocca…*: Jean-Louis Rocca, "Homeowners' Movements: Narratives on the Political Behaviours of the Middle Class." In Minglu Chen and David S.G. Goodman (eds), *Middle Class China: Identity and Behaviour*. Northampton: Edward Elgar, 2013, pp. 127–8.

102 *Just as the existing…*: See also Alvin Y. So and Su Xianjia, "New Middle Class Politics in China: The Making of a Quiet Democratization?" In Joseph Y.S. Cheng (ed.), *Whither China's Democracy? Democratization in China since the Tiananmen Incident*. Hong Kong: City University of Hong Kong Press, 2011.

105 *In Professor Li's…*: Li Gan, "Findings from the China Household Finance Survey." January 2013 (econweb.tamu.edu/gan/Report-English-Dec-2013.pdf; accessed November 22, 2013).

105 *Sociologist Yuval Elmelech…*: Yuval Elmelech, *Transmitting Inequality: Wealth and the American Family*. Lanham MD: Rowman & Littlefield, 2008, p. 147.

105 *Many economic…*: E.g. Maury Gittleman and Edward N. Wolff. "Racial Differences in Patterns of Wealth Accumulation." *Journal of Human Resources* 39 (1) (2004): 193–227.

105 *Economists…*: Darrick Hamilton and William Darity Jr. "Can 'Baby Bonds' Eliminate the Racial Wealth Gap in Putative Post-Racial America?" *Review of Black Political Economy* 37 (2010): 207–16; 212.

106 *In China…*: Li Liao, Nuonan Huang and Rui Yao. "Family Finances in Urban China." *Journal of Family Economic Issues* 31 (2010): 259–79.

106 *For these male…*: Bourdieu, *The Social Structures of the Economy*, p. 19.

FOUR

111 *"More property was… "*: Bettine Birge, *Women, Property and Confucian Reaction in Sung and Yuan China (960–1368)*. New York: Cambridge University Press, 2002, p. 2.

111 *"Often they owned… "*: Ibid., p. 3.

111 *Historian Kathryn Bernhardt…*: Kathryn Bernhardt, *Women and Property in China, 960–1949*. Stanford CA: Stanford University Press, 1999.

111 *Women's increased…*: Ibid., p. 12.

112 *"It is these women… "*: Ibid., p. 3.

112 *"References to 'daughters'… "*: Birge, *Women, Property and Confucian Reaction*, p. 91.

112 *Here, it is worth…*: ACWF and NBS Survey, "Di san qi zhongguo funü shehui diwei diaocha zhuyao shuju baogao."

112 *Birge writes that Song…*: Birge, *Women, Property and Confucian Reaction*, p. 95.

113 *"When the man died… "*: Ibid., p. 91.

113 *The special…*: Ibid., p. 138.

114 *Historian Dorothy Ko…*: Dorothy Ko, *Cinderella's Sisters: A Revisionist History of Footbinding*. Berkeley: University of California Press, 2007.

114 *The decisive turn…*: Birge, *Women, Property and Confucian Reaction*, p. 1.

114 *Women's property rights…*: Bernhardt, *Women and Property in China, 960–1949*.

115 *"If a sonless man… "*: Ibid., p. 42.

115 *"For a daughter… "*:. Ibid., p. 4.

115 *Since around twenty percent…*: Ibid., p. 43.

116 *The Qing state…*: Ibid., p. 4.

116 *Historian Susan L. Mann…*: Susan L. Mann, *Gender and Sexuality in Modern Chinese History*. Cambridge: Cambridge University Press, 2011.

117 *In the 19th century…*: Ibid., p. 4.

117 *These men…*: Ibid., p. 5.

117 *Mann describes…*: Ibid.

118 *Compare the mid-Qing…*: "30 sui yixia nanxing…." Xinhua. June 21, 2012.

118 *If the bride's family…*: Susan Mann, "Grooming a Daughter for Marriage: Brides and Wives in the Mid-Qing Period." In Susan Brownell and Jeffrey N. Wasserstrom (eds), *Chinese Femininities/Chinese Masculinities*. Berkeley: University of California Press, 2002.

119 *It was just prior…*: Lydia H. Liu, Rebecca E. Karl, and Dorothy Ko (eds), *The Birth of Chinese Feminism: Essential Texts in Transnational Theory*. New York: Columbia University Press, 2013.

119 *"No mere 'supplement'… "*: Ibid., p. 31.

119 *As a result…*: Ibid., p. 32.

120 *In her essay, "Economic Revolution… "*: Ibid., p. 97.

121 *"Ancient teaching… "*: Ibid., p. 128.

121 *He-Yin Zhen's indictment…*: Ibid., p. 36.

121 *A hundred years…*: Ibid., p. 21; Judith Butler, *Undoing Gender*. New York: Routledge, 1994.

121 *"The social system… "*: Liu et al., *The Birth of Chinese Feminism*, p. 53.

122 *"Chinese men… "*: Ibid., p. 55.

123 *"While the men… "*: Edwards, *Gender, Politics, and Democracy*, p. 62.

123 *Qiu Jin worked…*: Ibid., p. 63.

124 *"As such, Miss Zhao's predicament… "*: Karl, *Mao Zedong in the Twentieth Century World*.

124 *"China's intellectual… "*: Edwards, *Gender, Politics, and Democracy*, pp. 105–6.

124 *"In this, the lawmakers… "*: Bernhardt, *Women and Property in China, 960–1949*, p. 102.

125 *Yet even then…*: Ibid., p. 5.

125 *Historian Gail Hershatter…*: Gail Hershatter, *The Gender of Memory: Rural Women and China's Collective Past*. Berkeley: University of California Press, 2011, p. 4.

125 *Rural families were…*: Ibid., p. 109.

126 *Yet although women…*: Ellen R. Judd, "No Change for Thirty Years: The Renewed Question of Women's Land Rights in Rural China." *Development and Change* 38 (4) (2007): 689–710; 692.

127 *"In the fields… "*: Karl, *Mao Zedong in the Twentieth Century World*.

127 *Official rates…*: Gail Hershatter, *Women in China's Long Twentieth Century*. London: University of California Press, 2007.

127 *"Being liberated… "*: Guo Yuhua, speaking at "Contemporary Research on Chinese Women" workshop in Beijing, organized by CEFC, May 11, 2013; Guo Yuhua, "Xinling de jitihua: Shanbei Jicun nongye hezuohua de nüxing jiyi." *Social Sciences in China* 4 (2003): 48–61.

128 *"In the collectivist… "*: Guo, "Xinling de jitihua", ibid.

128 *"After working… "*: Guo speaking at "Contemporary Research on Chinese Women" workshop.

129 *The famine largely…*: Karl, *Mao Zedong in the Twentieth Century World*.

129 *In many parts…*: Sally Sargeson, "Why Women Own Less, and Why It Matters More in Rural China's Urban Transformation." *China Perspectives* 4 (2012): 35–42; Junjie Chen and Gail Summerfield, "Gender and Rural Reforms in China: A Case Study of Population Control and Land Rights in Northern Liaoning." *Feminist Economics* 13 (3–4) (2007): 63–92.

130 *In essence, women…*: Xiaoyun Li et al., "Gender Inequality and Poverty in Asset Ownership." *Chinese Sociology and Anthropology* 40 (4) (2008): 49–63.

130 *Sargeson finds…*: Sargeson, "Why Women Own Less."

130 *For example, not one…*: Xiaoyun Li et al., "Gender Inequality and Poverty in Asset Ownership."

131 *"It's the women who… "*: Sargeson, "Why Women Own Less," p. 38.

131 *A 17–province…*: Landesa 6th 17-Province China Survey. April 26, 2012.

131 *Sally Sargeson and…*: Sally Sargeson and Yu Song, "Land Expropriation and the Gender Politics of Citizenship in the Urban Frontier." *China Journal* 64 (July 2010).

132 *Sargeson documents…*: Sargeson, "Why Women Own Less."

132 *Moreover, the small…*: Ibid., p. 41.

132 *She finds that out of 343…*: Ibid.

In consequence, Sargeson concludes…: Ibid., p. 42.

133 *Anthropologist Yunxiang Yan…*: Yunxiang Yan, *Private Life Under Socialism.* Stanford CA: Stanford University Press, 2003.

133 *Yan focuses on…*: Ibid.

133 *"The younger sons… "*: Ibid.

134 *Yan writes that in spite of…*: Ibid.

134 Yan argues that "the new form of *ganzhe… "*: Ibid.

135 *As for the supposed…*: E.g. Katherine Trent and Scott J. South, "Mate Availability and Women's Sexual Experiences in China." *Journal of Marriage and Family* 74 (1) (2012): 201–14.

135 *"… what rights do rural women…"*: Sally Sargeson, "Women's Property, Women's Agency in China's 'New Enclosure Movement': Evidence from Zhejiang." *Development and Change* 39 (4) (2008): 645.

FIVE

140 *Government figures…*: ACWF and NBS Survey, "Di san qi zhongguo funü shehui diwei diaocha zhuyao shuju baogao."

143 *For example…*: Mieko Yoshihama, "A Web in the Patriarchal Clan System – Tactics of Intimate Partners in the Japanese Sociocultural Context." *Violence Against Women* 11 (10) (2005): 1236–62.

144 *Women's rights…*: Jianmei Guo and Li Ying. "Women's Rights Protection in China." In Indira Jaising (ed.), *Elusive Equality: Constitutional Guarantees and Legal Regimes in South Asia, Malaysia and China.* New Delhi: Women Unlimited, 2011, p. 231.

144 *"Considering that gender… "*: Ibid., p. 243.

146 *"Every year…"*: Feng Yuan, speaking at "Contemporary Research on Chinese Women" workshop in Beijing, organized by CEFC, May 11, 2013.

146 *The UN Multi-Country…*: *UN Multi-Country Study on Men and Violence in Asia and the Pacific.* September 2013.

147 *"The widely… "*: "Domestic Violence by Men 'Shocking': Survey." *China Daily.* May 10, 2013.

147 *In China's most famous…*: D.K. Tatlow, "In China's Most Watched Divorce Case, 3 Victories, 1 Defeat." *New York Times.* February 4, 2013.

157 *"It's a huge flaw…* ": Ibid.

158 *In his paper…*: Joshua Rosenzweig, "Disappearing Justice: Public Opinion, Secret Arrest and Criminal Procedure Reform in China." *China Journal* 70 (July 2013): 73–97; 96.

158 *For example, the Beijing…*: "Domestic Violence Highlighted as Women's Congress Concludes." *People's Daily* website. November 2, 2013.

159 *Medical researchers…*: Susan P.Y. Wong et al., "Understanding Self-Harm in Victims of Intimate Partner Violence: A Qualitative Analysis of Calls Made by Victims to a Crisis Hotline in China." *Violence Against Women* 17 (4) (2011): 532–44.

159 *Meanwhile, a 2009…*: Luo Ming et al. "Zhongguo nütong (shuang) xinglianzhe – Jiating baoli zhuangkuang diaocha baogao." *Tongyu.* January 2009.

160 *Legal scholar…*: Margaret Woo, "Shaping Citizenship: Chinese Family Law and Women." *Yale Journal of Law and Feminism* 15 (1) (2003): 99–134.

SIX

165 "Outside of…": Feng Yuan, speaking at "Contemporary Research on Chinese Women" workshop in Beijing, organized by CEFC, May 11, 2013.

166 *Li and other volunteers shaved their heads…*: D.K. Tatlow, "Women in China Face Rising University Entry Barriers." *New York Times.* October 8, 2012.

169 *Sociologists Ching Kwan Lee…*: Ching Kwan Lee and Yonghong Zhang. "The Power of Instability: Unraveling the Microfoundations of Bargained Authoritarianism in China." *American Journal of Sociology* 118 (6) (2013): 1475–1508.

170 *All district governments…*: Ibid., p. 1485.

175 *She cites…*: Sophia Woodman, "Law, Translation and Voice: The Transformation of a Struggle for Social Justice in a Chinese Village." *Critical Asian Studies* 43 (2) (2011): 185–210; 205.

176 *"I was tired…* ": P. Mooney, "China's Sex-Worker Warrior Ye Haiyan Fights for Prostitutes' Rights." *The Daily Beast.* July 31, 2012.

182 *"Some gay men…* ": "Millions of Wives Wed to Gay Men: Expert." *China Daily.* February 2, 2013.

185 *Eva Pils…*: T. Phillips, "Chinese Journalist Was 'Illegally Abducted' by Security Forces." *Telegraph.* August 5, 2013.

188 *Recent studies…*: Wei-Jun Jean Yeung and Shu Hu, "Coming of Age in Times of Change: The Transition to Adulthood in China." *ANNALS of the American Academy of Political and Social Science* 646 (2013): 149–71.

188 *Population specialists…*: Yong Cai and Wang Feng, "From Collective Synchronization to Individual Liberalization: (Re) emergence of Late Marriage in New Shanghai." Paper delivered at Population Association of America Annual Meeting, Princeton University, May 3–5, 2012 (http://paa2012.princeton.edu/papers/120544; accessed 23 November 2013).

188 *"At least for the highly…* ": Ibid., p. 4.

Index